James Aquila Spurlock

The Gospel of God as taught by his Holy Son and prophet,

Jesus Christ

James Aquila Spurlock

The Gospel of God as taught by his Holy Son and prophet, Jesus Christ

ISBN/EAN: 9783337101510

Printed in Europe, USA, Canada, Australia, Japan

Cover: Foto ©Lupo / pixelio.de

More available books at **www.hansebooks.com**

THE MASTER.

THE

GOSPEL OF GOD

AS TAUGHT BY HIS HOLY SON AND

PROPHET,

Jesus Christ.

God is Good, He is Just, He is Perfect.

COMPILED BY
JAMES A. SPURLOCK,
A LAWYER OF VERSAILLES, MO.

In Paper, Fifty Cents.
SOLD BY SPURLOCK & CO
Versailles, Mo.

Entered according to the Act of Congress **on the** 29th day of June,
A. D. 1894,
By JAMES A. SPURLOCK,
in the office of the Librarian of Congress, **at** Washington.

Table of Contents.

CHAPTER I.

Christ's sermon on the mount—Glory and power of God—His light, life and life of man—The Word—Truth—All born of God—All sons and daughters of God—All things made by him—Not born of the flesh—Two royal commandments—Are tests of all others—Penalty of violating them—Murder, direct and indirect—Stealing, direct and indirect—Adultery.

CHAPTER II.

Revenge forbidden—God no respecter of persons—God is love, and never curses any of his children at any time—Sobriety—Usury—Perfection—All on the way to heaven under God's care and majesty—Borrowing and lending—Feed the hungry, etc.—Swear not—Prayer—Not to pray until reconciled to brother—God's compassion on poor and ignorant—Alms—Lord's prayer—Forgive trespasses—Fasting—Cheerfulness enjoined—God is a spirit—His strength to save us.

CHAPTER III.

Covetousness — Contentment — Lay up treasures in heaven—Eye must be single unto God—Ye cannot serve God and mammon—Parable of the rich man and Lazarus—One in hell, the other in heaven—The rich farmer—Labor six days and provide for thine own—The Sabbath—Then take no covetous thought—Seek heaven first—Great reward in heaven for every day of labor—And laborers to have bright crowns—The idle to receive stripes in hell to hasten them to heaven.

CHAPTER IV.

Mercy—Judge not, condemn not—Grudge not—Forgive—The wicked servant—Cast into prison of hell—Do not err—No variableness in God—Examine yourselves—Cast the beam from thine eye—Seek the kingdom of heaven, ask, etc.—God better and more merciful than any man—Hypocrisy—Correct wrongs—Pay the laborer—Lend to neighbor—Good measure—The golden rule—Not a sparrow shall fall without God's perception and help—Hairs of head numbered—Nothing lost—Rewards of the righteous.

CHAPTER V.

Faith without works is dead—Charity the evidence of love and mercy—Shall cover many sins—Humility—Take low seats at feasts—Call the poor to your feasts—Use hospitality, but alike to rich and poor—How to act when the rich and poor visit you—Ye are convicted by the royal law if you have respect to persons—Call none father nor master—Love one another—No man hath seen God—God is love, love is truth—All variety compared to heaven—Love little children—The Father raises the dead, but does not judge them—Neither does Christ—They are self-adjudged by their works.

CHAPTER VI.

How to be saved—Keep the commandments—The good Samaritan—The greatest commandments—Wicked servants to be beaten with many stripes—The ignorant with few stripes—Are there few saved?—Narrow way and broad way—All to be saved finally—Marriage of the King's son—All that came, good and bad, had on wedding garments, except Satan—Not the Father's will that they should be lost—Blessings for the righteous—Woes for the wicked—God will draw all men to him—The good cannot repent for the bad—Christ is the door—Bad men cannot enter by other ways—A man cannot get religion—It must be by good works, which are treasures in heaven.

CHAPTER VII.

How to be saved—None good except God—The ten commandments—Give to the poor—Danger of riches—Sell that thou hast and give to the poor—Nothing impossible with

God—Jesus showeth that the publicans and harlots will go to heaven before the chief priests and elders—Life more abundant—Pray against temptation—The Pharisee and the publican pray in the temple—Exalt not thyself—Christ called little children and blessed them—None shall injure them—Charity and selfishness compared—Training of children—Every house builded by some man—Heaven and all things of God and are his children's—The silver rule—All flesh shall see the salvation of God—Not a sparrow to fall without his help—All saved and nothing to be lost—The flesh profiteth not—The *Word* is life eternal—God draws us to him.

CHAPTER VIII.

Repentance, how made—Just persons need no repentance—He that cometh to the Lord he will not cast out—Tree known by its fruits—Go to Christ, all ye that are weary and heavy laden—Be of good cheer—If ye do well, ye shall be accepted — All sins shall be forgiven, except blaspheming against the Holy Ghost—Revile not the gods—A man to reap that which he sows—He that damages his neighbor, let him make recompense—If he steals a hoe or any other thing, let him restore it—Kingdom of God at hand—Blight of sin—Love God—Fear Satan—Purify your souls—Humble yourselves—The infidel—Least in heaven greater than John the Baptist was here—Death shall come as a snare—The law of sacrifice was until John—God requires love, mercy, and charity—Rewards to righteous—Three great errors.

CHAPTER IX.

The prodigal son—He demanded his portion—Went into a far country—Wasted his portion—A famine came—He died—Was lost in hell—Was restored to his reason—Repented—Arose and went to his Father in heaven—His royal reception and feast—That reception and feast spread for all—God's great love to his children—He is omnipotent, yet cannot do all things at once—His warm invitation to all to come—False prophets slander God—The least has the most powerful friend in him—God is good—And will draw all men unto him, and gather them unto their fathers and mothers, even the wicked, in due time, and reward them as their works shall be—God is rich and ye are his heirs.

CHAPTER X.

Offenses— Drawing the sword—Forgiveness—Church differences—Forgive thy brother as often as he asks it—Who is Christ's brother?—Tradition of men, as washing cups and pots—Devouring widows' houses—Imposing heavy taxes and burdens—Unrighteous decrees—Gather not from the poor to scatter to the rich—Marriage and divorce—Adulterous woman —No marriages in heaven as in the world—All men, past and present, live unto God—Render to Cæsar and God their own— The widow's mite.

CHAPTER XI.

Death—New birth into heaven—Explained to Nicodemus—All shall know the voice of the Son of God—Death described—The angels shall appear—Shall take all to the judgment bar as soon as dead—Death swallowed up in victory —The judgment—Rewards to the righteous and wicked—This gospel to be preached so the world will have no cloak for its sins—Building house on rock and sand—Christ's poverty in this world's goods.

CHAPTER XII.

HEAVEN.

God created it and spread it out—Garnished it—He ruleth it—Many mansions—Each star a mansion—Full of angelic life—All good, clean, and beautiful—No marriages, pain, or sorrow there—Life is eternal—We will know each other— Angels travel and work—Work does not fatigue—All are young there—They are children of light, and they shine as the sun—They differ in glory, according to their works—Why we do not see them here—All are perfected there as their work shall be—God's voice fills the infinite heavens, cheering the angels—The mind cannot conceive the good things there— A star as bright as the morning star for the good—The sun and his planets our heaven—Nothing vile or unclean can enter heaven—The angels cannot get unclean—The raiment of the angels, peace and contentment.

CHAPTER XIII.

HELL AND THE EXILE.

Hell is a purgatory to remove sins—A school of instruction and repentance and cleansing—Sinners cleansed by God's love and righteousness, not by fire—The work is done by angels—Hell is the sinner's condition—First, second, and third divisions of hell—Repentance in hell—Finally each arises and goes to God, as they repent, until they all go—Necessity for a hell—God's love for sinners the same as a mother's love for her child—The land and the sea—Death and hell must give up their dead unto God—The angel of hell is his servant—The blight of sin after repentance—Falling short of the glory of God is eternal punishment.

THE EXILE.

Its nature—A matter of choice for some angels—Only the very wicked choose it—Blasphemy against the Holy Ghost—Such choose the exile—If a man is punished in this world, he will not be in the next—Angels in exile have all the feasts of heaven, and are contented.

CHAPTER XIV.

Christ's ministry—He sends out his disciples to preach—They return with joy—Jesus baptized not, but his disciples—He goes to the Feast of Tabernacles and preaches—Warned that Herod would kill him—Great multitudes hear him preach—The transfiguration of Christ to angel form—His glorious appearance—What he did during his ministry—He ordains his church—Gives St. Peter, his oldest apostle, the keys to heaven—Jesus and his disciples go to Jerusalem at the Feast of the Passover—They went by Jacob's Well to Bethany—There a supper was given them—Mary, the sister of Martha, anoints his head and feet against his death and burial—His triumphal entry into Jerusalem—He drove the money-changers from the temple with a scourge of small plaited ropes—He and his apostles eat the Passover—He instituted the sacrament of his supper—Washes his disciples' feet—He appoints Judas, and commanded him to betray him, and ordered him to do so quickly—Poor Judas humbly obeys his Master, and then hanged himself for grief.

CHAPTER XV.

Christ's farewell to his disciples—He cried and said, "I and my Father are one, but he is greater than I; he is greater than all"—All things made known to the disciples—He sends them to preach—Love and peace enjoined—Life in heaven—He to be cast out from this earth—"Be not troubled"—Ye shall live—He will draw all men unto him—The Holy Spirit of truth—False prophets—"Judge ye what is right, but err not"—Christ is the way—Follow him—God judges no man, nor Christ, but the law—Christ came from the Father and goeth again to him—"In our Father's house are many mansions"—Be not afraid, but cheerful in your tribulations—He promises to come again—His prayer for the world and disciples.

CHAPTER XVI.

Christ would not flee—His agony in the garden—His arrest—Peter cut off one of Malchus's ears—Christ healed it—He that taketh the sword shall perish by the sword—Peter denied Christ—Jesus was taken before the high priest—He avowed that he was Christ—Had spoken nothing in secret—An officer strikes Jesus—Crowing of the cock—Peter wept—Jesus taken before Pilate for trial—Judas was so grieved that he hanged himself—Jesus was tried first before Pilate, who acquitted him—On a demand by the priests, he was sent before Herod, who acquitted him—Pilate acquitted him again—But, for fear of Cæsar, Pilate delivered Jesus to be crucified—His crucifixion—His resurrection—On the cross he forgives his slayers—Committed his mother to John's care—At his death angels appear—Also at his resurrection and ascension.

CHAPTER XVII.

His ascension to heaven—His commissions to the women and disciples—Christ afterwards preaches to the spirits in hell—Makes a prison delivery—Conclusion of the whole matter—Love God and keep his commandments in thy strength and manhood as well as in sickness and old age.

EXPLANATION.

I have studiously endeavored to collect all the important commandments and promises of God to man, out of sacred history, into this work, and so arrange them that they be more readily found and better understood.

I have proceeded on the great truths, that God is good and merciful, and that there is no evil or spite in Him, and that He is the very best friend of man, whether they are good or bad; that hell is not a consuming fire, but is a fire of love, repentance, and instruction, in which the wicked are purified, taught, and prepared for heaven for all they are worth or can be made.

All the verses contained in this book, if not the very words of the present record, are strictly so in spirit, and are truth.

Some few will doubt, perhaps, the love and goodness of God as shown herein, but they will please remember that God is better than any man, however good and holy that man may be. Therefore doubt not, for all, good and bad, shall finally see the salvation of God and heaven, and be rewarded according to their works.

God in His majesty and goodness so loves all His children, good and bad, in this world, that He has commanded all men and nations not to kill, hurt, rob, falsely teach, condemn to hell, or injure them in the least; and if they are sick, to visit them; and if in want, to give them the necessaries of life without grudging—under the penalty of being cast into prison by their transgressions (not of God), and there to remain till they pay the last farthing; then they arise and go to their Father in heaven, and are rewarded for all good works.

A man shall reap that which he sows, and religion begins at the cradle and ends at the grave.

Death-bed repentance will not avail a man very much, as faith and prayer without works are dead. But they are good deeds and help him.

Ministers of the gospel and good people should visit the sick and the dying and comfort them with the goodness of God and heaven, for the very wicked and disobedient have many more good deeds to their credit in heaven than forgetful man can remember, and not one of the good deeds shall be forgotten by our Father in heaven, but each one of them shall be abundantly rewarded, as treasures laid up in heaven.

If a man does not try to keep the commandments of God and Christ, he does not believe in either of them or love them. It is folly for him to think so. Such words as "hell fire," "everlasting fire," "damnation or hell," "destruction," "perish," "wrath of God," "bottomless pit," "eternal punishment in hell," are used in this book to warn man of the evil and blight of sin. And the word "Me" as used by Christ oftentimes means "My Gospel," and "My Father," "Our Father." Follow His gospel, for His burden is light and His yoke is easy.

JAMES A. SPURLOCK,
May the 1st, 1895.　　　Versailles, Missouri.

CHAPTER I.

Christ's sermon on the mount—Glory and power of God—His light, life and life of man—The Word—Truth—All born of God—All sons and daughters of God—All things made by him—Not born of the flesh—Two royal commandments—Are tests of all others—Penalty of violating them—Murder, direct and indirect—Stealing, direct and indirect—Adultery.

1 Christ and his disciples went up into the Mount, and he chose his twelve apostles.

2 And he spake unto them and the multitudes that came to hear him, as man never spake before, saying:

3 God our Father created the starry heavens and the earth, and he said, *Let there be light, and there was light.*

4 In the beginning was the Word, and the Word was with God, and the Word was God.

5 The same was in the beginning with God.

6 All things were made by him, and without him not anything was made that was made.

7 In him there is life everlasting, and there is infinite strength in that life.

8 The life of God is the light of men, and the life of men is the light of God.

9 That light shineth in the darkness of our bodies and giveth us life through the will and power of God, and we comprehend it not.

10 We are not born of our own will, nor of the flesh, nor of the will of the flesh, nor of the will of man, but we are born of God.

11 *Ye are all brethren;* ye are all the sons and daughters of the true and living God.

12 He is the Father of all humanity, and loves

his children with tender mercy, and has the highest right to govern.

13 We are all members of his family, and are all members of his church, both good and bad.

14 He raises up the dead and quickens them with everlasting life in heaven.

15 Glory be to God in the highest, peace and good-will towards men.

16 I come not to destroy, but to fulfill the law and the prophets.

17 I come not to seek mine own honor, but the honor of our Father in heaven, who sent me. I receive not honor from men.

18 I come not to call the righteous, but sinners to repentance and knowledge of God.

19 I am sent to preach the gospel of God, and the kingdom of heaven to this world. I came into this world to bear witness unto the truth, that ye may have life in heaven more abundantly.

20 In the beginning God gave to man two great royal commandments. The first is,

21 THOU SHALT LOVE THE LORD THY GOD WITH ALL THY HEART, AND WITH ALL THY SOUL, AND WITH ALL THY MIND, AND WITH ALL THY STRENGTH.

22 The second is, THOU SHALT LOVE THY NEIGHBOR AS THYSELF.

23 On these two great royal commandments hang all the law and the prophets, and not a part of them.

24 All other laws are only explanatory of these two, and must be compared and tested by them.

25 Whatsoever is spoken, whatsoever is written, and whatsoever is done in accordance with these two commandments is truth.

26 And by the exercise or obeying the truth ye shall be saved in heaven.

27 And whatsoever is spoken, whatsoever is written, and whatsoever is done not in accordance with them is error; and for willful error, not repented of, you shall receive condemnation by the law.

28 Whosoever shall, knowingly and of his own will, break the least of these commandments, and teach men so, shall be called the least in the kingdom of heaven.

29. And whesoever shall do them, and teach men so, shall be called great in the kingdom of heaven; for all men, even the very wicked, shall in due time be drawn into the kingdom of heaven and be rewarded according to their works, but the condition of the very wicked will be very bad, in mind and body.

30 Ye have heard it said, Thou shalt not kill, that thou shalt do no murder, and that whosoever shall kill shall be in danger of the judgment.

31 But I say unto you, That whoever shall commit murder shall be held guilty of violating all the laws of God.

32 And whosoever shall injure his brother by word, act, deed, or evil contrivance shall be in danger of hell fire.

33 Ye are all brethren, and whosoever shall be angry with his brother without a cause, or shall say to him, Thou fool, or Thou worthless fellow, shall be in danger of the judgment.

34 There are many ways of killing a man and of stealing from him. It is not necessary to have a club, a dagger, nor a gun to kill him.

35 But he may be, and is most frequently, killed by the slow poison of human oppression: he or some member of his family.

36 One man or combination of men may so oppress another, and perhaps his family, that it is not possible for him or his family to procure food, raiment, and shelter.

37 Then they hunger first, they sicken next, and then die. This is like lying in wait and killing the victims, and is murder.

38 It would be better for a man if a mill-stone were first tied about his neck and he cast into the sea, than he be guilty of human oppression.

39 Ye have heard it said, Thou shalt not steal, nor defraud.

40 But I say unto you, That whosoever shall deprive his brother or his neighbor of his liberty, his labor, his lands, his house, his property, or just rights, by any species of fraud, cunning, or deceit, gambling, lying, cheating, usury, or unjust taxes, or contrivance or combination of men, stands convicted by the law of stealing and defrauding.

41 The only way to repent of stealing is to make recompense to the injured party in this life, or pay the last farthing in the prison of hell.

42 Ye have heard it said, Thou shalt not commit adultery. But I say unto you, Whosoever looketh on a woman to lust after her and encompass her shame and ruin hath already committed adultery in his heart.

43 And whosoever puts away his wife, except for the cause of adultery, committeth sin; and likewise with the wife if she do so.

44 The blackguards and profane swearers shall be known in the judgment by their mouths.

CHAPTER II.

Revenge forbidden—God no respecter of persons—God is love, and never curses any of his children at any time—Sobriety—Usury—Perfection—All on the way to heaven under God's care and majesty—Borrowing and lending—Feed the hungry, etc.—Swear not—Prayer—Not to pray until reconciled to brother—God's compassion on poor and ignorant—Alms—Lord's prayer—Forgive trespasses—Fasting—Cheerfulness enjoined—God is a spirit—His strength to save us.

1 Ye have heard it has been said of olden times, An eye for an eye, and a tooth for a tooth. But I say unto you, Bear with one another, and render not evil for evil, or railing for railing, but contrariwise blessings.

2 Ye have heard that it has been said, Thou shalt love thy neighbor, and hate thine enemy.

3 But I say unto you, Love thine enemies, bless them that curse you, do good to them that hate you, and pray for them which despitefully use and persecute you,

4 That ye may have a great reward in the kingdom of heaven. These texts overrule one-half of the teachings of the ancients and much of the present day.

5 God is no respecter of persons, nor partial to any, but has reserved judgment and rewards to be made and rendered in heaven. He knows no more of the great priests, ministers, and rulers of this earth than he knows of the humble people. They are all his own children.

6 He maketh his sun to shine on the evil and the good, and sendeth his rain on the just and the unjust.

7 If ye salute your brethren only, or love them only which love you, what do ye do more than others?

8 If your brother offend thee, forgive him, for he will repent in this world, or in the next, and finally meet thee in heaven.

9 God is love, and is far exalted in heaven above any hatred, malice, spite, or revenge, and never at any time cursed or hated any of his children, but loves all of them, and will in due time exalt all of them in the kingdom of heaven.

10 God is a spirit, and must be worshiped in spirit and truth by all true worshipers.

11 Be ye sober, be ye steadfast, and if sinners entice thee, consent thou not. Strive to be perfect as your Father in heaven is perfect.

12 Ye are all brethren, both good and bad, pursuing life's journey to the judgment-bar of heaven under the sure and mighty dispensation of God, where every one shall be judged and rewarded as his works shall be.

13 Therefore avoid giving offences one to another, but have ye compassion one to another.

14 Love as brethren: Be courteous. Imagine no evil against thy neighbor.

15 Eschew evil and do good. Seek peace and pursue her ways. Bridle thy tongue from evil, and let thy lips speak no guile or falsehood.

16 Thou shalt not take usury nor interest for the loan or forbearance of money or commodity, except paid by free consent of the borrower.

17 But if thou borrowest, pay it back with reasonable interest, if you reasonably can.

18 Thou shalt not refuse to lend thy neighbor

the necessaries of life, however poor or trifling he may be.

19 Thou shalt feed the hungry, clothe the naked, visit the sick with proper relief, if needed, and those in prison, and entertain the stranger or cause it to be done; all these thou shalt reasonably and righteously do.

20 Ye have heard it said, Thou shalt perform all thine oaths unto the Lord, and not forswear thyself.

21 But I say unto you, Swear not at all; neither by heaven, for it is God's throne; nor by the earth, for it is his footstool; neither by thy head, because thou canst not make one hair white or black.

22 Let your communications be, Yea, yea; or Nay, nay: for more than these may come of evil.

23 Thou shalt love and honor thy father and thy mother. He that hateth his father, his mother, his wife, his child, his brother, his sister, his neighbor, or his own life, cannot be my disciple, and cannot be worthy of the kingdom of heaven till he loves them, and he shall love God more than these.

24 When ye pray, forgive, if ye have aught against anyone, that your Father in heaven may forgive you.

25 When thou shalt come before the altar of prayer, remember if thy brother or sister hath aught against thee. If so, make not that prayer; but go first and be reconciled to thy brother or sister, and then come and make thy prayer.

26 Agree with thine adversary quickly, while thou art in the way of life with him, lest at any time he shall accuse thee before the judge, and the judge deliver thee to the officer, and thou be cast into the prison of hell.

27 Verily I say unto thee, Thou shalt by no means come out from thence till thou hast paid the uttermost farthing.

28 But God will have compassion for the ignorant, poor, and weak.

29 Take heed that ye do not your alms before men, to be seen of them; if ye do, ye have no reward in heaven.

30 Therefore when thou doest thine alms, do not sound a trumpet before thee, as the hypocrites do, that they may have glory of men. Verily I say unto you, They have their reward.

31 But when thou doest thine alms, let not thy left hand know what thy right hand doeth,

32 That thy alms may be in secret, and thy Father which seeth in secret himself shall reward thee openly in heaven.

33 And if thou doest thy neighbor a kind deed, thou shalt not cause him to acknowledge the same before men.

34 When thou prayest, thou shalt not be as the hypocrites are, for they love to pray standing in the houses of worship, and in the corners of the streets, that they may be seen of men. Verily I say unto you, They have their reward.

35 But when thou prayest, enter into thy closet, and when thou hast shut the door, pray to thy Father which is in secret, and he shall reward thee openly in heaven.

36 When ye pray, use not vain repetitions, as the heathen do; for they think they shall be heard for their much speaking.

37 Be not like unto them, for your Father knoweth what things ye have need of before ye ask of him.

38 After this manner therefore pray ye: OUR FATHER WHICH ART IN HEAVEN, HALLOWED BE THY NAME.

39 THY KINGDOM COME. THY WILL BE DONE IN EARTH AS IT IS IN HEAVEN.

40 GIVE US DAY BY DAY OUR DAILY BREAD.

41 FORGIVE US OUR TRESPASSES AS WE FORGIVE THOSE WHO TRESPASS AGAINST US. FORGIVE US OUR DEBTS AS WE FORGIVE OUR DEBTORS.

42 SUFFER US NOT TO BE LED INTO TEMPTATION, BUT DELIVER US FROM EVIL. FOR THINE IS THE KINGDOM, THE POWER, AND THE GLORY, FOR EVER. AMEN.

43 For if ye forgive men their trespasses, your heavenly Father will also forgive you your trespasses.

44 But if ye forgive men not their trespasses, neither will your heavenly Father forgive you your trespasses. Strive to be merciful as your Father in heaven is merciful.

45 When ye fast, be not as the hypocrites are of a sad countenance; for they disfigure their faces that they may appear unto men to fast. Verily I say unto you, They have their reward.

46 But when thou fastest, wash thy face and anoint thy head, and be of cheerful countenance, that thou appear not unto men to fast, but unto thy Father in secret, and thy Father shall reward thee openly in heaven.

47 Fear not, but be ye cheerful in all well-doing, and despond not in health or sickness.

48 For ye have a friend of great strength and

power in heaven, even your Father in heaven, who careth for you, and will finally draw you into his kingdom and reward you most bounteously for every good work you have done in this life.

49 All must be finally drawn into the kingdom of heaven and receive all the rewards and joy they can contain, for it is God's will, pleasure, and providence, be the rewards much or little.

50 Doubt not. For the power of God unto the salvation of every creature of this earth into heaven is at hand, and thy heaven is in thy sight, and there is room provided there for all.

51 God's power is within you and surrounds every one of you, as the waters of the sea surround the fishes, and nothing can be lost forever, however small, weak, or feeble it may be.

52 God helps all equally, and does not punish any, even the child in its mother's womb, nor man in the course of his life through this world.

53 Every pain and ache of mortal flesh is God's strength drawing us to heaven; but woe unto that man who interferes with the love, mercy, and justice of God, for he shall abase himself in the kingdom of heaven.

CHAPTER III.

Covetousness — Contentment — Lay up treasures in heaven — Eye must be single unto God — Ye cannot serve God and mammon — Parable of the rich man and Lazarus — One in hell, the other in heaven — The rich farmer — Labor six days and provide for thine own — The Sabbath — Then take no covetous thought — Seek heaven first — Great reward in heaven for every day of labor — And laborers to have bright crowns — The idle to receive stripes in hell to hasten them to heaven.

1 Thou shalt not covet nor defraud.

2 Take heed and beware of covetousness; for a man's life consists not in the abundance of things he possesses in this world.

3 Be contented with such things as ye have, till ye have more by honest industry and care.

4 Thou shalt not covet anything that belongs to thy neighbor, nor even try to defraud him out of it. But ye may purchase it at a fair price, if it is property only.

5 Lay not up for yourselves treasures on earth, where moth and rust doth corrupt, and where thieves break through and steal.

6 But lay up for yourselves treasures in heaven, where neither moth nor rust doth corrupt, and where thieves do not break through nor steal.

7 For where your treasure is, there will your heart be also.

8 Ye are the children of light. The light of thy body is the eye. Therefore if thine eye be single unto righteousness, thine whole body shall be full of the light of God.

9 But if thine eye be evil, thy whole body shall be full of darkness. If therefore the light that

is in thee be darkness, how great is that darkness!

10 Men love darkness rather than light because their deeds are evil.

11 No man can serve two masters; for he will hate the one and love the other, or he will hold to the one and despise the other.

12 Ye cannot serve God and mammon. That which is highly esteemed among men is often an abomination in the sight of God.

13 There was a certain rich man, which was clothed in purple and fine linen, and who fared sumptuously every day.

14 And there was a certain beggar named Lazarus, which was laid at his gate, full of sores,

15 And desiring to be fed with the crumbs which fell from the rich man's table.

16 But he would not. Moreover, the dogs came and licked his sores.

17 And it came to pass that the beggar died, and was carried by the angels into Abraham's bosom in heaven.

18 And the rich man also died, and he was buried.

19 And in hell he lifted up his eyes, being in torment, and seeth Abraham afar off, and Lazarus in his bosom.

20 And he cried, and said, Father Abraham, have mercy on me, and send Lazarus, that he may dip the tip of his finger in water and cool my tongue, for I am tormented in this flame.

21 But Abraham said, Son, remember that thou in thy lifetime receivedst good things, and likewise Lazarus evil things; but now he is comforted and thou art tormented.

22 And besides all this, there is a great gulf

fixed (the law) between us, so that they that would pass from hence to you cannot, neither can they pass to us, from thence, that would come.

23 Then he said, I would pray thee, father, that thou wouldst send him to my father's house, for I have five brethren, that he may testify unto them, lest they come to this place of torment.

24 And Abraham said unto him, They have Moses and the prophets; let them hear them.

25 And he said, Nay, Father Abraham; but if one went unto them from the dead they will repent.

26 And he said unto him: If they hear not Moses and the prophets, neither will they be persuaded though one rose from the dead.

27 This rich man was lost in the first division of hell, because he had murdered his own brother by refusing to feed him and give him shelter in his sickness and poverty, and for like crimes.

28 A certain rich man's ground brought forth plentifully, and he thought within himself, saying, What shall I do? because I have no room where to bestow my fruits.

29 And he said, This I will do: I will pull down my barns and build greater, and there will I bestow my fruits and goods.

30 And I will say unto my soul, Soul, thou hast much goods laid up for many years; take thine ease; eat, drink, and be merry. But God said unto him, Thou fool, this night thy soul shall be required of thee; then whose things shall those be that thou hast provided?

31 So it is; he that layeth up treasure for himself is not rich towards God.

32 By the sweat of thy brow thou shalt earn thy bread.

33 Six days shalt thou labor, and do all thy work and provide for thine own, but the seventh day is the Sabbath day of the Lord thy God.

34 Remember the Sabbath day to keep it holy; works of charity and necessity are (only) allowed.

35 These thou shalt do. Then take no covetous thought for your life, what ye shall eat; nor for the body, what ye shall wear.

36 This life is more than the meat, and the body is more than the raiment.

37 Consider the ravens; they neither sow nor reap, and which have neither storehouse nor barn and God feedeth them.

38 How much more are ye better than the birds? and which of you by taking thought can add one cubit to his stature?

39 And if ye be not able to do that thing which is least, then why take thought for the rest?

40 Consider the lilies, how they grow; they toil not, neither do they spin. Yet I say unto you, That Solomon in all his glory was not arrayed like one of these.

41 If, then, God so clothed the grass, which is to-day in the fields, and to-morrow is cast into the oven, how much more will he clothe you, O ye of little faith?

42 Take no covetous thought for to-morrow, for what ye shall eat, drink, or wear; neither be ye of doubtful minds. Sufficient unto the day is the evil thereof.

43 Seek ye first the kingdom of God, and his love and righteousness, and all these things shall be added unto you.

44 Sell that ye have and give alms to t he poo

and the needy. Provide yourselves with bags that wax not old, a treasure in heaven that faileth not. What is a man profited if he shall gain the whole world and lose his own soul? or what shall a man give in exchange for his soul?

45 The rich men, unless they repent and make recompense for their transgressions in this life, shall weep and howl in their last day; for their miseries shall come upon them in the judgment.

46 Their gold and silver shall be cankered, their fine raiment moth-eaten, and their oppression of the poor, and the first fruits of the harvest which they have withheld from the husbandman, shall rise up as witnesses against them.

47 Covet not, but do thy reasonable share of labor in this world. Then trust God, but fear murderers, thieves, robbers, and liars.

48 For every day a man or a woman shall labor in this world at useful labor they shall receive one million years happy enjoyment in heaven. Yea, more.

49 The man shall outshine any of the kings of this earth, and the woman any of the queens of this earth, in heaven.

50 The command to labor is imperative, so far as to provide for his or her own, and is the most pleasing and acceptable way of worshiping our heavenly father.

51 But the lazy and the idle, who will not do their reasonable share of useful work when they can, shall be lost in the second division of hell, and there beaten with stripes, many or few, to awaken them into action, so they may repent and love and serve God, when they will be exalted to the third and last,

and highest division of hell, in which the prodigal son was lost.

52 There they complete their repentance, and go to paradise, which is the second division of heaven, where all is love, happiness, and joy forever more.

CHAPTER IV.

Mercy—Judge not, condemn not—Grudge not—Forgive—The wicked servant—Cast into prison of hell—Do not err—No variableness in God—Examine yourselves—Cast the beam from thine eye—Seek the kingdom of heaven, ask, etc.—God better and more merciful than any man—Hypocrisy—Correct wrongs—Pay the laborer—Lend to neighbor—Good measure—The golden rule—Not a sparrow shall fall without God's perception and help—Hairs of head numbered—Nothing lost—Rewards of the righteous.

1 Judge not, that ye be not judged.

2 Condemn not, lest ye be condemned. For God in his mercy will not suffer a feeble and blind man to judge and condemn to hell anyone.

3 If a sinner commits sin, thou mayest reprove the sin, but thou shalt not condemn the soul of that sinner to hell.

4 Grudge not, one against another, lest ye be condemned. Give to the needy without grudging.

5 He shall have judgment without mercy that hath showed no mercy.

6 A servant of a certain king owed him ten thousand talents and was not able to pay. The servant fell down and worshiped him, saying, Lord, have patience with me, and I will pay thee all.

7 And the lord of that servant was moved with compassion and loosed him and forgave him the debt.

8 But the same servant went out and found one of his fellow-servants who owed him a hundred pence, and he laid hands on him and took him by the throat, saying, Pay me that thou owest me.

9 And his fellow-servant fell down at his feet and besought him, saying, Have patience with me, and I will pay thee all.

10 And he would not, and went and had him cast into prison till he should pay the debt.

11 So when his fellow-servants saw what was done, they were very sorry, and came and told their lord what was done.

12 Then his lord, after he had called him, said unto him, O thou wicked servant, I forgave thee all that debt at thy request.

13 Should not thou have had compassion on thy fellow-servant, as I had pity on thee.

14 And his lord was wroth and delivered him to the tormentors till he should pay all that was due unto him.

15 So likewise shall our heavenly Father do unto you also, if ye, from your hearts, forgive not every one his brother their trespasses.

16 Do not err. Every good and perfect gift is from God, the Father of light, in whom there is no variableness, neither show of turning.

17 Be ye doers of the word, and not hearers only, deceiving yourselves. There is one law-giver, O feeble man: even God, who is able to destroy. Who art thou that judgeth another?

18 Why beholdest thou the mote that is in thy brother's eye, and considereth not the beam that is in thine own?

19 Or how wilt thou say to thy brother, Let me pull the mote out of thine eye, while a beam is in thine own eye?

20 Thou hypocrite, first pull the beam out of thine own eye, and then thou shalt see more clearly to pull the mote out of thy brother's eye.

21 Examine yourselves and see that ye are not in error. Confess your faults, one to another.

22 Implore pardon one of another for wrongs

done. Seek the kingdom of heaven, and ye shall find it; knock, and it shall be opened unto you.

23 Ask and ye shall receive. Ask, whatever ye will, and it shall be given you.

24 For every one that asketh receiveth, and he that seeketh findeth, and to him that knocketh it shall be opened.

25 What man is there of you, whom if his son ask bread, will give him a stone? or if he ask a fish, will give him a serpent? or if he ask for an egg, will give him a scorpion?

26 IF YE THEN, BEING EVIL, KNOW HOW TO GIVE GOOD GIFTS UNTO YOUR CHILDREN, HOW MUCH MORE SHALL YOUR FATHER WHICH IS IN HEAVEN GIVE GOOD THINGS TO THEM THAT ASK HIM?

27 Be not deceivers and hypocrites. There is nothing covered that shall not be revealed, and neither hidden that shall not be made known.

28 Whatever ye have spoken in the ear, in closets, shall be proclaimed from the housetops.

29 If thou hast done wrong or injury to thy neighbor or his property of any kind, correct it without delay, and refrain from it in the future.

30 The laborer is worthy of his hire, and the ox is worthy of his feed. If thy neighbor or a stranger serve thee, thou shalt pay him before the sun goeth down, if he needs it, and thou shalt not oppress him.

31 Lend to thy neighbor, expecting nothing in return for the use of the loan. But if thou borrowest from him, pay it back with good measure.

32 Leave off all usury and extortion, and retore to every one his own.

33 For with what measure ye measure unto others, it shall be again measured unto you in heaven.

34 Love and honor thy rulers as they love and honor you. Thy rulers shall impose no unjust burdens on you, nor suffer the people of this world to be despoiled by *usury, extortion*, or combines of men against them.

35 THEREFORE, IN ALL THINGS WHATSOEVER YE WOULD THAT MEN SHOULD REASONABLY AND RIGHTEOUSLY DO UNTO YOU, DO YE EVEN SO UNTO THEM, FOR THIS IS THE LAW AND THE PROPHETS AND THE GOLDEN RULE OF HEAVEN.

36 It shall be observed at all times and in all places and in all conditions. Every plant not planted of God shall be rooted up.

37 Are not two sparrows sold for a farthing? and not one of them is forgotten before God, or shall fall unnoticed by him.

38. *Fear not, therefore; ye are of more value than many sparrows.* Even the very hairs of your head are numbered, and not one of them shall be lost.

39 He that knoweth the word of God and shall keep it to the best of his ability shall bear much fruit, some thirty, some sixty, and some one hundred fold, in heaven.

40 Blessed are they that hear the word of God and keep the same as best they can.

41 Blessed is he that resisteth temptation and beareth his cross in this world, for his reward in heaven shall be great.

42 Blessed is he that earneth his bread by the sweat of his brow, for his measure and joy in heaven shall be great and full.

CHAPTER V.

Faith without works is dead—Charity the evidence of love and mercy—Shall cover many sins—Humility—Take low seats at feasts—Call the poor to your feasts—Use hospitality, but alike to rich and poor—How to act when the rich and poor visit you—Ye are convicted by the royal law if you have respect to persons—Call none father nor master—Love one another—No man hath seen God—God is love, love is truth—All variety compared to heaven—Love little children—The Father raises the dead, but does not judge them—Neither does Christ—They are self-adjudged by their works.

1 If thou believeth there is one God, thou doest well.

2 If thou hast faith in him to keep his commandments, then thy faith is sufficient; and if thou hast not, then pray God to increase your faith, for devils believe and tremble.

3 What doth it profit a man if he hath faith and hath not works? Faith cannot save him if he hath not works of love and charity.

4 If a brother or a sister be naked, and destitute of daily food, and one of you say unto them, Depart ye in peace; be ye warmed, be ye filled, and ye give them not those things needful to the body, what doth it profit thee?

5 Even so, if faith hath not works, it is dead, being alone.

6 Show me thy faith without thy works, and I will show you my faith by my works.

7 For without faith, love, mercy, and charity it is impossible to please God.

8 For as the body without the spirit is dead, so faith without works is dead also.

9 If any be a hearer of the word and not a doer, he is deceived. Be ye doers of the word, and not hearers only. He that hath love hath charity; and he that hath not love and faith hath not sufficient charity and good works.

10 Charity shall cover, or make recompense for, a multitude of sins.

11 A man does not love or believe in God and Christ till he believes in their comandments and promises and makes an honest effort to keep them to the best of his ability. He is not required to do things he cannot do.

12 All men are a thousand-fold better than most people believe them to be. The farmer, the mechanic, the laborer, and the teachers of the young are much more important men and women than their rulers, and much better on this earth.

13 Now abideth faith, hope, and charity; but of these three, charity is the greatest.

14 Open wide thy hand to thy brother, the poor and the needy. Lend of that thou hast and give to them, for ye have the poor with you always.

15 Happy shall ye be in heaven if ye do these things.

16 Humble yourselves in the sight of God, and he shall lift you up with his mighty hand in due time. Cast all your care on him, for he loveth and careth for you.

17 When thou art bidden of any man to a wedding or a feast, sit not down in the highest room or seat, lest a more honorable man than thou be bidden of him.

18 And he that bade you and him come and say unto thee, Give this man place; and thou begin with shame to take the lowest room.

19 But when thou art bidden, go and sit down in the lowest room or seat, that when he that bade thee cometh, he may say unto thee, Friend, go up higher. Then thou shalt have honor in the presence of them that sit at meat with thee.

20 When thou makest a feast, dinner or supper, call not thy rich friends, but call the poor, the maimed, the lame, the blind, and thou shalt be blessed; for they cannot recompense thee, and thou shalt be recompensed at the resurrection of the just.

21 Use hospitality one to another without grudging, for God loves a cheerful giver.

22 If there come into thine house or assembly a man with a gold ring and arrayed in fine apparel, and there also cometh a man in poor apparel, thou shalt not say to him in rich apparel, Sit thou here in my best place, and then say unto him in poor apparel, Stand thou there, or, Sit here on my footstool.

23 For if ye do, ye have respect of persons and commit sin, and are convicted by the law as transgressors.

24 If ye fulfill the royal law of God, thou shalt love thy neighbor as thyself.

25 If thou art called to judge a matter, thou shalt not lean to the rich.

26 For God resisteth the proud and giveth grace to the humble.

27 Love not gorgeous apparel nor the uppermost rooms and seats at feasts, nor chief seats in the churches, nor greetings in the markets.

28 Neither be ye called master, for ye are all brethren and one is your Master in heaven. Ye are all the children of God.

29 Neither call ye any father, for one is your Father in heaven.

30 For he that would be greatest among you shall be your servant in heaven. Even as the Son of God came not to be ministered unto, but to minister.

31 Verily I say unto you, The servant is not greater than the master; neither is the disciple greater than the lord; neither is he that is sent greater than him which sent him.

32 I command you that ye love one another, as I have loved you.

33 No man hath seen God at any time. If ye love one another, God dwelleth in you, and his love is perfected in you.

34 There is no fear in love, for perfect love casteth out fear.

35 God is love, and he that dwelleth in love dwelleth in God, and God in him.

36 By this we know we love the children of God—when we love God and keep his commandments. If ye love God, keep his commandments, and ye will the best ye can.

37 If a man says he loves God and hateth his brother, he is deceived. He who loveth God loveth his brother also. Love not in word or speech, but in deed and truth.

38 Whosoever hath this world's goods and seeth his brother or sister hath need of them, and shutteth up his bowels of compassion from them, hath not the love of God in him.

39 If thy heart condemneth thee, God is greater than thy heart and knoweth all things. Love not the world nor the things that are in the world,

for if any man love them, he is a servant of mammon and the love of the Father is not in him.

40 For all that is in this world, the lust of the flesh, the lust of the eyes, and the pride of this life, is not of the Father, but of the world, and the world passes away, and the lusts thereof, but he that doeth the will of the Father abideth in heaven forever.

41 Take heed that ye love and despise not one of these little children, for I say unto you, That in heaven their angels do always behold the face of my Father which is in heaven.

42 By the love of God ye know the spirit of truth and the spirit of error.

43 The Father loveth the Son, and showeth to him all things that himself doeth.

44 And as the Father raiseth up the dead and quickeneth them, even so the Son quickeneth whom he will.

45 The Father judgeth no man, but hath committed all judgment unto the Son. I judge not of myself. As I see and hear, I judge with tender love and mercy, and so do the angels.

46 But of mine ownself I do nothing, but by my Father which sent me. I receive not honor from men, and if I bear witness of mine ownself without the help of God, my witness is not true.

47 I speak as I am commanded by the Father, and my words are truth and life everlasting.

CHAPTER VI.

How to be saved—Keep the commandments—The good Samaritan—The greatest commandments—Wicked servants to be beaten with many stripes—The ignorant with few stripes—Are there few saved?—Narrow way and broad way—All to be saved finally—Marriage of the King's son—All that came, good and bad, had on wedding garments, except Satan—Not the Father's will that they should be lost—Blessings for the righteous—Woes for the wicked—God will draw all men to him—The good cannot repent for the bad—Christ is the door—Bad men cannot enter by other ways—A man cannot get religion—It must be by good works, which are treasures in heaven.

1 And behold a certain lawyer stood up tempting Christ, saying, Master, what shall I do to inherit eternal life? And he said unto him, What is written in the law? How readest thou?

2 And the lawyer answering said, Thou shalt love the Lord thy God with all thy heart, and with all thy soul, and with all thy strength, and with all thy mind; and thy neighbor as thyself.

3 And he said unto him, Thou hast answered right. This do and thou shalt live.

4 But the lawyer, willing to justify himself, said, Who is my neighbor?

5 And Jesus answered and said, A certain man went down from Jerusalem to Jericho, and fell among thieves, which stripped him of his raiment and wounded him, and departed leaving him half dead.

6 And by chance come down a certain priest that way, and when he saw him he passed by on the other side.

7 And likewise a Levite, when he was at the place, came and looked on him, and passed by on the other side.

8 But a certain **Samaritan**, as he journeyed, come where he was, and he saw him, and had compassion on him, and went to him, and bound up his wounds, pouring in oil and wine, and set him on his beast and brought him to an inn, and took care of him.

9 And on the morrow, when he departed, he took out two pence and gave them to the host, and said unto him, Take care of him, and when I come again I will repay thee whatever thou spendest more.

10 Which of these three, thinkest thou, was neighbor unto him that fell among the thieves?

11 And the lawyer said, He that shewed mercy. Then Jesus said unto him, Go thou and do likewise.

12 A scribe came and asked Jesus, saying, Which is the greatest commandment?

13 And Jesus answered him, saying, The Lord thy God is one Lord, and thou shalt love the Lord thy God with all thy heart, and with all thy soul, and with all thy mind, and with all thy strength. This is the first commandment.

14 And the second is like unto it, namely, Thou shalt love thy neighbor as thyself. There is none other commandment greater than these.

15 The scribe said, Well, Master, thou hast said the truth. And Jesus said, Thou art not far from the kingdom of heaven.

16 That servant that knew his master's will and prepared not himself nor did according to his will shall be beaten with many stripes, but he that knew not and did commit things worthy of stripes shall be beaten with few stripes.

17 For unto whomsoever much is given, of him much is required. And to whom men have committed much, of him they will ask the more.

18 Be ye ready, for the Son of man cometh at an hour when ye think not. Then said one to him, Lord are there few saved? And he said unto them, Strive to enter in at the strait gate, for many, I say unto you, shall seek to enter in thereat and shall not be able.

19 For wide is the gate and broad is the way that leadeth to destruction, and many go in thereat.

20 Because strait is the gate and narrow is the way which leadeth unto perfect life, and few there be that find it.

21 But every one that is perfect shall be as the Master. And they shall come from the east and the west, and from the north and the south, and sit down in the kingdom of heaven, but shall not all be perfect, as they are rewarded as their works shall be.

22 And behold there are last which shall be first in perfection, and there are first which shall be last. But all will finally come, when they are perfected and taught of God, but only for what they are worth.

23 The kingdom of heaven is like unto a king which made a marriage for his son and sent forth his servants to call them that were bidden to the wedding, and they would not come.

24 And he sent forth other servants to call them that were bidden, saying, I have prepared my dinner, and all things are ready. Come unto the marriage.

25 But they made light of it and went their way, one to his farm, one to his merchandise, and some entreated his servants despitefully.

26 Then he saith to his servants, They which were bidden were not worthy. Go ye therefore

into the highways and hedges, and so many as ye shall find, bid to the marriage.

27 So those servants went out into the highways and hedges, and gathered all, including the poor, the maimed, the halt, and the blind, as they could find, both good and bad, and the wedding was furnished with guests.

28 And when the king came to see the guests, he saw there one, a man, that had not on a wedding garment, Satan.

29 And he said unto him, Friend, how camest thou in here not having on a wedding garment? And he was speechless.

30 Then the king said unto his servants, Bind him and cast him into outer darkness.

31 Fear not, for it is not the will of your Father in heaven that one of the least of you shall be forever lost, for ye are members of his church and of his family.

32 All shall be saved in the kingdom of God, though they are thousands of years repenting and learning to obey the laws of God, in hell.

33 God will surely draw all men unto himself in heaven, through repentance in this world or in the next.

34 The harvest is great and the laborers are few. Pray ye therefore to the Lord of the harvest to send more laborers to the harvest. There are many called and few chosen.

35 Blessed are the dead, for they all live in heaven unto God, and are rewarded according to their works.

36 Blessed be ye poor, for yours is the kingdom of God.

37 Blessed are ye that hunger now, for ye shall be filled.

38 Blessed are the just, for they shall be given a crown of glory.

39 Blessed are they that mourn, for they shall be comforted.

40 Blessed are the meek, for they shall inherit the earth.

41 Blessed are the merciful, for they shall obtain mercy.

42 Blessed are the charitable, for their joy in heaven shall be full.

43 Blessed are they who hunger and thirst after righteousness, for they shall be filled.

44 Blessed are the pure in heart, for they shall see God.

45 Blessed are the peacemakers, for they shall be called the children of God.

46 Blessed are the righteous, for they shall shine forth as the sun in the kingdom of their Father. He that hath ears let him hear.

47 Blessed are they who are persecuted for righteousness' sake, and blessed are ye when men persecute you for my sake.

48 Rejoice and leap for joy, for great is your reward in heaven, for so persecuted they the prophets.

49 Let your light so shine before men that they may see your good works and glorify your Father which is in heaven.

50 But woe unto you that are rich. Ye have your consolation and fill.

51 Woe unto you that are full, for ye shall hunger.

52 Woe unto you that laugh now, for ye shall mourn and weep.

53 Woe unto you when all men speak well of you, for so did their fathers to the false prophets.

54 Woe unto the wicked; unless ye all repent in this life, ye will be damned in the next life.

55 For a good man cannot repent or suffer for a bad man's sins, and a bad man cannot take a good man's reward and joy away from him.

56 I and my commandments are the door to everlasting salvation and life in heaven, and he that tries to climb up by ways other than this door, the same is a thief and a robber.

57 And Jesus said unto those that believed, If ye continue in my *word*, then ye are my disciples in deed.

58 And ye cannot get religion by faith and prayer alone, without works of love, mercy, and charity, and the more of these works the better.

59 And the less of religion a man has, the more apt he is to fight over it.

60 Every good deed a man does for his fellow-man is a treasure laid up in heaven that he can never lose, and it endureth forever to his honor and glory.

61 Why call ye me Lord, Lord, and do not the things which I say?

62 Ye shall be saved, in heaven, by keeping my commandments, and rewarded accordingly.

CHAPTER VII.

How to be saved—None good except God—The ten commandments—Give to the poor—Danger of riches—Sell that thou hast and give to the poor—Nothing impossible with God—Jesus showeth that the publicans and harlots will go to heaven before the chief priests and elders—Life more abundant—Pray against temptation—The Pharisee and the publican pray in the temple—Exalt not thyself—Christ called little children and blessed them—None shall injure them—Charity and selfishness compared—Training of children—Every house builded by some man—Heaven and all things of God and are his children's—The silver rule—All flesh shall see the salvation of God—Not a sparrow to fall without his help—All saved and nothing to be lost—The flesh profiteth not—The *Word* is life eternal—God draws us to him.

1 And behold one came and said unto Jesus, Good Master, what good things shall I do, that I may have eternal life?

2 And he said unto him, Why callest thou me good? There is none good save one, that is God: but if thou wilt enter unto life, keep the commandments.

3 And he saith unto him, Which? Jesus said, The two royal commandments are:

I. THOU SHALT LOVE THE LORD THY GOD WITH ALL THY HEART, AND WITH ALL THY SOUL, AND WITH ALL THY MIND, AND WITH ALL THY STRENGTH.

And the second is like unto it; namely:

II. THOU SHALT LOVE THY NEIGHBOR AS THYSELF.

4 And the ten commandments are:

I. I am the Lord thy God, and thou shalt have no other gods before me; thou shalt not make unto thee any graven image, nor any likeness, nor bow thyself down to them, nor serve them.

II. Thou shalt not take the name of the Lord thy God in vain.

III. Remember the Sabbath day, to keep it holy.

IV. Six days shalt thou labor and do all thy work, and provide for thine own. But the seventh day is the Sabbath day of the Lord thy God; in it thou shalt not do any work.

V. Honor thy father and thy mother.

VI. Thou shalt not kill or do any murder.

VII. Thou shalt not commit adultery.

VIII. Thou shalt not steal nor defraud.

IX. Thou shalt not lie, nor bear false witness.

X. Thou shalt not covet anything that is thy neighbor's.

5 The young man saith unto him, Master, all these things have I kept from my youth up. What lack I yet?

6 And Jesus saith unto him, If thou will be perfect, go and sell that thou hast, and give to the poor, and thou shalt have treasure in heaven, and come and follow me, or keep my commandments.

7 But when the young man heard that saying, he went away sorrowful, for he had great possessions.

8 Then Jesus said unto his disciples, Verily I say unto you, That a rich man shall hardly enter into the kingdom of heaven.

9 It is easier for a camel to go through the eye of a needle, than for a rich man to enter into the kingdom of God.

10 But Jesus said, With men this is impossible, but with God all things are possible.

11 Jesus saith unto the chief priest and elders,

What think ye? A certain man had two sons: and he came to the first and said, Son, go work to-day in my vineyard.

12 And he answered and said, I will not; but after he repented and went.

13 And he came to the second and said likewise, and he answered and said, I go, sir; and he went not.

14 Whether of the twain did the will of his father?

15 They say unto him, The first. Jesus saith unto them, Verily I say unto you, That the publicans and the harlots go into the kingdom of God before you.

16 For John came unto you in the way of righteousness and ye believed him not; but the publicans and harlots believed him.

17 And ye, when ye had seen it, repented not, afterwards, that ye might believe him.

18 I am come that ye might have life, and have life more abundantly. Watch and pray, that ye enter not into temptation; the spirit is indeed willing, but the flesh is weak.

19 There is life, and life more abundant, and perfect life in the kingdom of heaven.

20 Two men went up into the temple to pray, the one a Pharisee and the other a publican.

21 And the Pharisee stood and prayed thus, with himself, God, I thank thee that I am not as other men are, extortioners, unjust, adulterers, or even as this publican. I fast twice a week and give tithes of all I possess.

22 And the publican, standing afar off, would not lift up so much as his eyes unto heaven, but

smote on his breast, saying, God be merciful to me a sinner.

23 I tell you, this man went down to his house justified rather than the other.

24 For every one that exalteth himself shall be abased, and he that humbleth himself shall be exalted.

25 And they brought unto him infants that he would touch them. But when his disciples saw it, they rebuked them.

26 But Jesus called them unto him and said, Suffer little children to come unto me, and forbid them not, for of such is the kingdom of heaven.

27 Verily I say unto you, Whosoever shall not receive the kingdom of God as a little child, he shall not enter therein.

28 And he took them up in his arms, put his hands on them, and blessed them.

29 If any man desire to be first, he shall be last of all, and servant of all, and a servant of servants in heaven.

30 And Jesus again took a child and set him in the midst of them, and when he had taken him in his arms, he said unto them,

31 Whosoever receiveth one of such children in my name receiveth me, and whosoever receiveth me receiveth not me, but him that sent me.

32 And whosoever shall offend one of these little ones that believe in me, by making its condition in life more intolerable or by rendering its pathway to heaven more difficult,

33 It is better for him that a millstone were first hanged about his neck and he were cast into the sea.

34 Whosoever shall give a loaf of bread, or a

cup of water, to one of the least of these of mine, in the spirit of a disciple, or brotherly love, verily, verily, I say unto you, He shall in no wise lose his reward.

35 Charity and good deeds shall give grace and strength to thine angel in heaven:

36 While selfishness and evil deeds shall fasten disgrace and weakness on thee in heaven.

37 Train thy children in the ways of righteousness, of faith, of virtue, of knowledge, of temperance, of patience, of love, of mercy, of brotherly kindness, and of charity;

38 And they shall neither be barren nor unfruitful in the kingdom of heaven. Train up a child in the way he should go, and he will not depart from it when he is old.

39 Every house is builded by some man; but he that built all things is God. This earth and the fullness thereof are His; and not any man's, except so far as his need of it demands.

40 Blessed is the man that endureth temptation, for when he is tried he shall receive the crown of life which God has promised to them that love him. Bear with each other's faults and infirmities.

41 Follow not that which is evil, but that which is good. Whatsoever ye would not have others do unto you, do not so unto them. This is the silver rule. Mercy unto you, and peace and love be multiplied.

42 For ye all have one Father, and ye are the sons and daughters of the living God, and it is not your Father's will that any of you shall be lost.

43 All flesh shall see the salvation of God through his love and tender mercies. But everyone shall be rewarded as his works shall be. All things

are God's, and not a sparrow shall fall without God's help.

44   This is the Father's will that sent me, that of all he hath given me, I should lose nothing, but should raise it up again at the last day.

45   It is the Spirit that quickeneth, the flesh profiteth nothing after death. The Word is life eternal. No man can come to God except he draws him to heaven.

46   The kingdom of God is within you, giving you life and giving you reason, and you shall improve that reason, and strengthen thy soul by good works in this life.

CHAPTER VIII.

Repentance, how made—Just persons need no repentance—He that cometh to the Lord he will not cast out—Tree known by its fruits—Go to Christ, all ye that are weary and heavy laden—Be of good cheer—If ye do well, ye shall be accepted — All sins shall be forgiven, except blaspheming against the Holy Ghost—Revile not the gods—A man to reap that which he sows—He that damages his neighbor, let him make recompense—If he steals a hoe or any other thing, let him restore it—Kingdom of God at hand—Blight of sin—Love God—Fear Satan—Purify your souls—Humble yourselves—The infidel—Least in heaven greater than John the Baptist was here—Death shall come as a snare—The law of sacrifice was until John—God requires love, mercy, and charity—Rewards to righteous—Three great errors.

1 Again I say unto you, I came not to call the righteous, but sinners to repentance.

2 They that are whole need not a physician, but they that are sick. Just persons need no repentance.

3 I tell you sinners, Except ye repent, ye shall all perish. Seek the Lord while he may be found.

4 Let the wicked man forsake his ways and the unrighteous man his thoughts, and take up his cross and follow me, and God will abundantly pardon him.

5 To-day if you will hear my voice, harden not your hearts, incline your ear unto me, hear and obey, and your souls shall live.

6 And he that cometh unto me I will in no wise cast out, and it shall come to pass that all that calleth on the name of the Lord shall be saved.

7 Come unto me, all ye that labor and are heavy laden, and I will give you rest.

8 Take my yoke upon you, and learn of me,

for I am meek and lowly of heart; and ye shall find rest to your souls,

9 For my yoke is easy, and my burden is light.

10 Be of good cheer, and let not your countenances be fallen. If thou doest well, thou shalt be accepted; and if thou doest not well, then sin lieth at thy door.

11 He that is not with me is against me, and he that gathereth not with me scattereth abroad.

12 Either make the tree good and its fruit good, or else make the tree corrupt and its fruit corrupt.

13 For the tree is known by its fruits. And the angels in heaven are known by the works, and works of love and charity are to thy soul as good soil and gentle rains to the tree, and a man's good deeds are his treasures in heaven.

14 What doth the Lord require of thee, but to do justly, and to love mercy, and to walk humbly with thy God?

15 I say unto you, All manner of sins and blasphemy shall be forgiven unto men, but blasphemy against the Holy Ghost, which is sin done to thy neighbor. Your bodies are temples of the Holy Ghost.

16 It shall not be forgiven him in this world, nor in the world to come, except by that neighbor.

17 Thou shalt not revile the Lord thy God, nor any of his lesser gods or angels.

18 O ye wicked, how can ye, being evil, speak good things? for of the abundance of the heart the mouth speaketh.

19 A good man, out of the treasure of his heart, bringeth forth good things; and an evil man, out of the evil treasure, bringeth forth evil things.

20 Speak not evil, one of another. Behold how good and pleasant for brethren to dwell together in unity.

21 If any man seem to be religious, and bridleth not his tongue, but deceiveth his heart, that man's religion is in vain. Wherefore, let every one be swift to hear, slow to speak, and slow to wrath.

22 Behold, how great a matter a little fire kindleth.

23 I say unto you, For every idle word men shall speak, they shall give an account thereof in the day of judgment.

24 For there is nothing covered that shall not be revealed; neither hid that shall not be known.

25 Therefore, whatsoever ye have spoken in darkness shall be heard in the light, and that which ye have spoken in the ear, in closets, shall be proclaimed upon the housetops.

26 Be not deceived. God is not mocked, for that which a man soweth shall he reap. If he soweth to the flesh, he shall reap corruption.

27 And if he soweth to the spirit, he shall reap life everlasting in heaven.

28 And if a man soweth sparingly, he shall reap sparingly; and if he soweth abundantly, he shall reap abundantly. And if a man shall preach salvation sparingly, he shall reap it sparingly. What shall your harvest be?

29 Repent ye, for there is more joy in heaven over one sinner that repenteth than over ninety and nine just persons which need no repentance.

30 Humble yourselves under the mighty hand of God and keep his commandments, and he will exalt you in due season.

31 If any shall steal his neighbor's hoe, his ax,

his money, or other property, let him restore it to the owner.

32 If any shall damage his neighbor or his property, his person or good name, let him make recompense for it the best he can.

33 And then pray God to forgive him his trespasses, and deliver him from evil in the future.

34 Why will some men believe, and teach, that a man may repent in this world in a few hours by faith, sorrow, and prayer, and that in a comfortable place, and then deny the sinner that right forever when he is in the flames, stripes, and hunger of hell? That is neither just nor merciful, and is not the law of God. Any man might well be ashamed to teach such doctrine, for it is a slander against God and the angels. The law is, *All flesh shall see the salvation of God*, through his tender mercies, and his tender mercies endureth forever.

35. There is no such thing as repentance or the pardon of sins in this world, except by the utmost effort to make recompense for the injury and evil done, unless the injured party forgives the evil done him. Then God will forgive, for he is much better than any man, however good that man may be.

36. If sins could be removed from the wicked by faith, prayer, and sorrow, without any effort to make recompense, then man will not be rewarded according to his works, whether they be good or evil. But that is the law of heaven and earth.

37 If a man cannot make recompense, the injured brother shall forgive him upon confession of his wrongs, and apology for them. Otherwise the sin will lie at his door.

38 For God will not abase or dishonor a man

who tries to do right, and by no means for his feebleness and poverty.

39 There are three great errors. The first is that God cursed Adam and Eve in the beginning for a slight disobedience, and also the earth for their sins.

40 The second is, that God kept angry with man for nearly four thousand years, and then sent his holy and beloved Son into this world to die and become a sacrifice for the sins of the world.

41 The third is, if a man shall believe in Jesus Christ, his death and resurrection, that he can be saved by faith and prayer, without works, and even with very wicked works.

42 These are all errors, and the transgressor and the heathen should not believe them, for God will surely reward every man according to his works, whether they are good or evil, and this reward cannot be changed by sacrifice. Watch what ye preach to the sinners and to the heathen.

43 God will have mercy, and not sacrifice; and he never cursed Adam and Eve, nor this earth, nor sent his Son to die for our sins in this world. He is far above such works, and there was no need for either of them.

44 The kingdom of God is at hand. Repent ye and believe and obey the gospel. God's commandments are not grievous to be borne, and the way of the transgressor is hard, for he will not hold the wicked guiltless.

45 Purify your souls through truth and love and good works while in this life; if not, they shall be in hell. Love God and fear him not, but fear the blighting effects of sin on your souls, which endureth forever.

46 Draw nigh unto God, and he will draw nigh

unto you. He is your very best friend. Resist Satan, and he will flee from you. He is your very worst enemy. He is a self-snatcher, and will snatch away your glory in heaven, if he can. *Watch him.*

47 Let none of you suffer as a murderer, as a thief, as an extortioner or oppressor of the weak or poor, nor as a busybody in other people's affairs.

48 Do not injure anyone by word, act, or deed, but submit yourselves to God and keep his commandments, and ye shall have abundant life in heaven. A man's sins cast him down to hell, under the law, and not God.

49 But if a man deny God with great swelling words in this world, and honor men for advantage, he shall appear before him in his kingdom as a man with but little knowledge, scarcely knowing his kindred or friends.

50 Verily, I say unto you, Among men born of women there hath not arisen a greater than John the Baptist; but the least in the kingdom of heaven is greater than he was on this earth.

51 Repent ye; for death shall come as a snare upon all men, and then shall appear the Son of man in the glory of his Father, with his holy angels, and then shall be *rewarded every man according to his works.**

52 Not everyone that sayeth unto me in that day, Lord, Lord, shall enter into the kingdom of heaven, but he that doeth the will of our Father in heaven to the best of his ability and opportunity.

53 For our Father shall have mercy on such

---

* The parable of the laborer, Matthew xx. 1, does not conflict with this text, for the laborers were ready all day and willing to work, and did work when called, and were entitled to full pay. It would have been different if they had been in the service of mammon or Satan eleven hours of that day. So with the Christian, if he is ready to serve God when duty calls him, and does so.

as are ignorant and out of the way, and on the feeble and the poor.

·54 And in that day the righteous shall shine forth as the sun in the kingdom of their Father. Be ye also ready. He that hath ears let him hear.

55 The law of sacrifices was until the day of John the Baptist; since that the law of the kingdom of God is preached, and all men should press into it.

56 Ye can no longer repent by making sacrifices of burnt offerings or other sacrifices;

57 For God will have love, mercy, and charity, and not sacrifices.*

58 John the Baptist baptised with water unto repentance.

59 But Christ baptised with the Holy Ghost and with fire unto salvation, by teaching the people of this world to love God and his angels in heaven, and man on this earth.

60 Watch ye and pray, lest ye enter into temptation. The spirit truly is ready, but the flesh is weak.

61 Shun and resist strong drink, for it shall bring you into poverty, want, and wretchedness in this world, and abase you in the life to come, for it is your worst enemy; fear it.

---

*See Ephesians ii. 8, 9. The word "works," as used there, means works of sacrifice or burnt offerings, and not works of love, charity, and righteousness. If it did, it would contradict Christ and his apostles.

CHAPTER IX.

The prodigal son—He demanded his portion—Went into a far country—Wasted his portion—A famine came—He died—Was lost in hell—Was restored to his reason—Repented—Arose and went to his Father in heaven—His royal reception and feast—That reception and feast spread for all—God's great love to his children—He is omnipotent, yet cannot do all things at once—His warm invitation to all to come—False prophets slander God—The least has the most powerful friend in him—God is good—And will draw all men unto him, and gather them unto their fathers and mothers, even the wicked in due time, and reward them as their works shall be—God is rich and ye are his heirs.

1 Christ said, A certain man had two sons. And the younger of them said unto his father,

2 Father, give me the portion of goods that falleth to me. And the father, in the goodness of his heart, divided unto them his living.

3 And not many days afterwards the younger son gathered all together and took his journey into a far country, and there he wasted his substance in riotous living.

4 And when he had spent all his living, there arose a mighty famine in that land, and he began to be in want.

5 And he went and joined himself to a citizen of that country, and he sent him into his fields to feed swine.

6 And he fain would have filled himself with the husks and bran that he fed to the swine, he was so hungry. And no man gave unto him.

7 In his want and humiliation he came to himself. And when he came to himself and was restored to his reason, he remembered his father.

8 And he said, I know that in my father's house there is plenty for him and for all his servants, and bread to spare for me and for all that shall come, while I perish with hunger here.

9 I will arise and go to my father, and I will say unto him, Father, I have sinned against heaven and before thee,

10 And I am no longer worthy to be called thy son; make me as one of thy hired servants.

11 And he arose, barefooted, and went to his father. But when he was yet a great way off, his father saw him and had compassion,

12 And ran with joy and met him. On meeting, the son said to him, Father, I have sinned against heaven and before thee, and I am no longer worthy to be called thy son.

13 But the father would not hear more, but fell upon his neck and kissed him.

14 And he said to his servants, Here is my son that was dead, and now he is alive; here is my son that was lost, and now he is found.

15 Bring forth the best raiment and put it on him, and put a ring on his hand and shoes on his feet.

16 Bring forth the fatted calf and kill it, and make him a feast and invite the guests.

17 And let us eat and be merry, for my son is alive and safely at home.

18 And they began to eat and be merry, and music and dancing was heard in that house.

19 And that feast is prepared in heaven, and the same welcome and joy for all that shall come.

20 For the good first, the indifferent next, and finally the wicked, though they repent in hell.

21 For God loves his children with all his heart, and with all his soul, and with all his mind, and

with all his majestic power, mercy, and goodness, and it is impossible for any to be forever lost.

22 And ye, in your feebleness, should love and honor God in like manner; and love thy neighbor as thyself.

23 But remember, while God is omnipotent and able and willing to save all his children in heaven, both good and bad, he is not omnipotent in all things at once.

24 For instance, he cannot make corn or wheat grow on a frozen lake, without first changing the conditions of that lake.

25 Neither can he bring a sinner, with a cold, icy heart, into his kingdom of heaven, without first changing the conditions of that heart.

26 He must first give the sinner a warm heart of love, mercy, humility, and charity.

27 This is repentance, and then the sinner can arise and go to him as the prodigal son did, and receive the like royal reception, feast, and banquet.

28 Be of good cheer and be patient, for ye are all under the mighty providence of God, and will, every one, be saved in heaven in due time, though ye repent for your crimes in hell for thousands of years.

29 For it is not your Father's will that any, even the least of you, shall be forever lost.

30 Neither is it his will that ye shall come to him through hell, but straight to heaven if ye will, for all may if they will.

31 God has all things prepared for you, and daily invites you to come.

32 The Spirit and the Bride say, Come; and let him that heareth say, Come; and let him that is hungry or athirst come; and whosoever will, let

him come and partake of the waters of life and feasts of heaven freely.

33 Beware of false prophets, which come to you in sheep's clothing, but inwardly they are as ravening wolves.

34 Ye shall know them by their fruits.

35 They have gone where God hath not sent them and taught evil of him.

36 They have slandered him by saying he was wicked and a God of malice and revenge, and spiteful to his children, and caused his people to err.

37 Follow them not, but keep my commandments, for God only is good and able to save and bless the people of this world in heaven.

38 Let the unmerciful man not condemn his neighbor forever, for that neighbor is his brother, and hath a more powerful and good friend, his Father in heaven, than he believes.

39 And besides this, that unmerciful man's curses availeth nothing in the kingdom of God.

40 For God is good, and has provided rest in heaven for all his children according to their merits, and his goodness, love, and abundant mercy.

41 The powers of heaven are pleasingly inviting you to come. The powers of earth are buffeting you and telling you to go. And all must soon arise and go to heaven, and there be most bounteously rewarded for every good deed they have done in this world.

42 God and heaven have attraction for the souls of men like this earth has for matter; and when the souls of men are released from the flesh by death of the body, they will be drawn to God and heaven, as vegetation and trees are drawn upwards into the light.

43 This attraction is stronger than the life of the natural body of man, and all souls that ever were, or are now, or ever will be on this earth, have been and will be drawn into heaven.

44 And this is truth: Even if the wicked are drawn through hell for purification, repentance, and instruction, yet they are never perfected as the righteous and just are.

45 Ye shall all be gathered unto your Father in heaven—the wicked, the just, and the good; but the first named shall be last, and the last named shall be first.

46 Ye shall be drawn there by the powers of God and of heaven, and there rewarded, each one according to his deeds and merits, but all in abundance.

47 And ye cannot go to the kingdom of God until your Father in heaven draw you there.

48 And ye will surely be drawn there, as heavy stones are drawn back to earth when thrown upwards, and even more so.

49 *If ye, being evil, know how to give good gifts to your children, how much more shall your heavenly Father give to them that ask him?*

50 All will finally be given all the joy they can contain, whatever their measure may be. And it is the will of your Father in heaven that ye bear much fruit, or good works. He is glorified if ye do.

51 *God is rich*, and ye are *his heirs* to all ye can contain of *his riches*.

52 Look to the planets, stars, and adamantine suns, and you will see of your inheritance and glory in heaven.

CHAPTER X.

Offenses — Drawing the sword—Forgiveness—Church differences—Forgive thy brother as often as he asks it—Who is Christ's brother?—Tradition of men, as washing cups and pots—Devouring widows' houses—Imposing heavy taxes and burdens—Unrighteous decrees—Gather not from the poor to scatter to the rich—Marriage and divorce—Adulterous woman—No marriages in heaven as in the world—All men, past and present, live unto God—Render Cæsar and God their own—The widow's mite.

1 Then said Jesus to his disciples, It is impossible but that wars and offenses will come, but woe unto him through whom they come. For he that draweth the sword shall perish by the sword.

2 It were better for him that a millstone were first hanged about his neck and he cast into the sea, than that he should offend one of these little ones, and make no recompense.

3 Take heed to yourselves. If thy brother trespass against thee, rebuke him; and if he repent, forgive him.

4 Tell him his faults between thee and him alone. If he hear thee, thou hast gained thy brother.

5 If he will not hear thee, then take with thee one or two more, that in the mouth of two or three witnesses every word may be established.

6 And if he shall neglect to hear them, tell it unto the church; but if he neglect to hear the church, let him be unto thee as a heathen man and publican.

7 And if thy brother trespass against thee seven times in a day, and turn again to thee and say, I repent, thou shalt forgive him.

8 Then Peter said unto him, Lord, how oft shall my brother sin against me and I forgive him? till seven times?

9 Nay, I say not unto thee, Till seven times; but, Until seventy times seven.

10 Where two or three are gathered together in my name, I will be in the midst of them.

11 Whosoever shall do the will of my Father which is in heaven, the same is my brother, and sister, and mother.

12 Then came the scribes and Pharisees and said unto Jesus, Why do thy disciples transgress the traditions of the elders? for they wash not their hands when they eat bread. But he answered and said unto them, Why do ye also transgress the commandment of God by your tradition?

13 Well did Esaias prophesy of you, saying, This people draweth nigh unto me with their mouths, and honoreth me with their lips, but their heart is far from me.

14 But in vain they do worship me, teaching for doctrines the commandments of men.

15 For laying aside the commandments of God, ye hold the tradition of men, as the washing of pots and cups, and many other such like things.

16 From the heart proceedeth evil thoughts, murders, thefts, fornication, covetousness, wickedness, deceit, filth, blasphemy, and evil eye, pride, and foolishness.

17 All these things come from within and defile the man, and not such things as he eats.

18 But woe unto you scribes and Pharisees. Ye shut up the kingdom of heaven against men, for ye neither go in yourselves, nor suffer ye them that are entering to go in.

19 Ye devour widows' houses, and for a pretense make long prayers; therefore ye shall receive the greater damnation.

20 Ye compass sea and land to make one proselyte; and when he is made, ye make him two-fold more the child of hell than yourselves

21 Woe unto you scribes and Pharisees; for ye pay tithes of mint and anise, and have omitted the weighty matters of the law, judgment, mercy, love, and faith. These ye have not done.

22 Ye are blind guides, which strain at a gnat and swallow a camel. Ye make clean the outside of the cup and platter, but within they are full of extortion and excess.

23 Ye also appear outwardly righteous unto men, but within ye are full of hypocrisies and iniquities.

24 Behold your house is left unto you desolate.

25 Woe unto you law-makers, for ye laid men with burdens grievous to be borne, and ye yourselves touch not the burdens with one of your fingers.

26 Woe unto them that decree unrighteous decrees, and impose grievous burdens upon others. Woe unto them that deprive the poor of their rights, that make widows their prey, and rob the fatherless, and impose on the weak and unfortunate.

27 Woe unto you when ye gather from the poor and scatter unto the rich; for ye should gather from the rich, rather, and scatter to the poor. How can ye escape the damnation of hell except ye repent and serve God in spirit and truth?

28 The Pharisees asked, Is it lawful for a man to put away his wife? tempting him; and Jesus answered them, What did Moses command you?

29 And they said, Moses suffered to write a bill of divorcement, and put her away.

30 And Jesus answered and said unto them, For the hardness of your heart he wrote you this precept.

31 But, from the beginning of the creation, God created them male and female; and for this cause a man shall leave his father and mother and cleave to his wife, and likewise doeth the wife.

32 And the twain shall be one flesh, so they are no more twain, but one flesh.

33 What, therefore, God hath joined together let no man put asunder.

34 The scribes and Pharisees brought in a woman taken in adultery, and say unto Jesus, Master, this woman was taken in adultery.

35 And now the law of Moses commanded us that such should be stoned, but what saith thou?

36 Jesus saith unto them, He that is without sin among you, let him first cast a stone at her.

37 And her accusers, being convicted by their own consciences, went out one by one, and Jesus was left alone, and the woman standing in the midst.

38 And Jesus said unto her, Woman, where are thine accusers? Hath no man condemned thee?

39 She said, No man, Lord. And Jesus said unto her, Neither do I condemn thee. Go, and sin no more.

40 Ye judge after the flesh. I judge no man; yet if I judge him, my judgment is true, for I am not alone, but I and the Father that sent me.

41 Whosoever committeth sin is the servant of sin. Ye shall know the truth, and the truth shall make you free.

42 No man, having put his hands to the plow and looking back, is fit for the kingdom of God.

43 Then came the Sadducees, which say there is no resurrection, and ask Jesus, saying,

44 Now there were seven brethren, and the first took a wife and died, and the second took her and died, and the third likewise.

45 And the seven had her, and last of all the woman died also. In the resurrection whose wife shall she be of them? for the seven had her to wife.

46 Jesus answered and said unto them, The children of this world marry and are given in marriage. In the resurrection they neither marry nor are given in marriage; neither can they suffer nor die any more, for they are equal unto the angels, and are the children of God, being the children of the resurrection.

47 The dead are raised; God is not a God of the dead, but of the living. All men, past and present, live unto God.

48 And then the Pharisees took counsel, that they might entangle Jesus, and they asked him, saying, Tell us, is it lawful to pay tribute to Cæsar?

49 And Jesus said, Why tempt ye me? Show me the tribute money. And they brought him a penny. And he saith unto them, Whose is this image and superscription? They say unto him, Cæsar's. Then saith he unto them, Render therefore unto Cæsar the things that are Cæsar's, and unto God the things that are God's.

50 When they heard these words, they marvelled and went away. Jesus looked up and saw the rich casting their gifts into the treasury.

51 And he saw also a certain poor widow casting in thither two mites.

52 And he said, Of a truth this poor widow hath cast in more than they all:

53 For all of these have cast in of their abundance, but she of her penury hath cast in all she had.

CHAPTER XI.

Death—New birth into heaven—Explained to Nicodemus—All shall know the voice of the Son of God—Death described—The angels shall appear—Shall take all to the judgment bar as soon as dead—Death swallowed up in victory—The judgment—Rewards to the righteous and wicked—This gospel to be preached so the world will have no cloak for its sins—Building house on rock and sand—Christ's poverty in this world's goods.

1 Verily, verily, I say unto you, The hour is coming, and now is, when the dead shall hear the voice of the Son of God, and they that hear shall live.

2 The dead shall come forth: they that have done good, unto the resurrection of life; and they that have done evil, to the resurrection of damnation.

3 As the Father hath life in himself, so he has given to the Son of man to have life in himself; and because I have life, thou shalt live also.

4 Jesus said, Destroy the temple of my body, and I will build it up again in three days.

5 Verily I say unto you, Except a man be born again, he cannot enter the kingdom of God in heaven.

6 And Nicodemus, a ruler of the Jews, saith unto him, How can a man be born again when he is old? Can he enter a second time into his mother's womb and be born again?

7 And Jesus answered, Verily, verily, I say unto thee, Except a man be born of water and of the Spirit, he cannot enter into the kingdom of God.

8 That which is born of the flesh is flesh, and that which is born of the Spirit is spirit.

9 Marvel not that I say, Ye must be born again.

10 The wind bloweth where it listeth, and thou hearest the sound thereof, but canst not tell whence it cometh or whither it goeth; so is every one that is born of the Spirit.

11 And Nicodemus said unto him, How can these things be? And Jesus said, Verily, verily, I say unto thee, We speak that which we do know, and testify that we have seen, and ye receive not our witness. And no man hath ascended up to heaven except he came from heaven, even the Son of man which is in heaven.

12 The hour is come that the Son of man should be glorified.

13 Except ye be converted and become as little children, ye shall not enter into the kingdom of heaven.

14 Verily I say unto you, Except a corn of wheat fall into the ground and die, it abideth alone; but if it die, it bringeth forth much fruit: some thirty, some sixty, and some a hundred fold.

15 What shall your harvest be?

16 Life is even as a vapor which appeareth for a little while and then vanisheth away.

17 A woman, when she is in travail, hath sorrow because her hour is come; but as soon as she is delivered of the child, she remembereth no more the anguish for joy that a man is born into the world.

18 Then shall there be great tribulations when ye are born again into the kingdom of heaven, and as the lightning cometh out of the east and

shineth even unto the west, so shall also the coming of the Son of man be into thee.

19 In your patience possess ye your souls, for there shall not a hair of your head perish.

20 Immediately after the tribulation of those days shall the sun be darkened, and the moon shall not give her light, and the stars shall fall from heaven, and the powers of heaven shall be shaken, as it were. The golden bowl shall be broken, and the silver cord of life loosened, and the temple of thy body shall be broken and laid low.

21 The Lord giveth, and the Lord taketh away; blessed be the name of the Lord.

22 Wheresoever the body is, there will be the eagles gathered together.

23 The flesh profiteth nothing then. And wheresoever a newborn soul is, there shall be the angels also.

24 It is the Spirit that quickeneth.

25 Then shall appear the sign of the Son of man in heaven, and he shall send his angels, nurses, guides, and comforters in white shining raiment, and with countenances as lightning, and as with a great sound of a trumpet.-

26 They shall say unto thee, Soul, arise; come with us to the kingdom of heaven.

27 In that day thou shalt be with me in paradise.

28 The body to dust, the soul to heaven.

29 Death shall be swallowed up in victory, and God will wipe away all tears from all faces, and all sorrow from all hearts.

30 O death, where is thy sting? O grave, where is thy victory?

31 And as one star differeth from another in glory, so shall the children of the resurrection.

32 Thus shall be gathered all the nations of the earth, from the uttermost parts of the earth to the uttermost parts of heaven.

33 Be ye ready and watch, for ye know not what hour your Lord doth come.

34 Who then is a faithful and wise servant whom the Lord has made ruler over his household, to give them meat in due season.

35 Blessed is that servant whom his Lord, when he cometh, shall find waiting and prepared.

36 Verily I say unto you, He shall make him ruler over all he hath.

37 He shall hear the welcome plaudit, Well done, thou good and faithful servant. Thou hast been faithful over a few things; I will make thee a ruler over many. Enter thou into the joy of thy Lord.

38 But if that evil servant shall say in his heart, My Lord delayeth coming, and shall begin to beat the men servants and maidens, and to eat and drink, and be drunken with gluttons and drunkards,

39 The Lord of that servant shall come in a day when he looketh not for him, and in an hour when he is not aware, and he will cut him asunder, and will appoint him his portion with the unbelievers and hypocrites.

40 What I say unto you, I say unto all, Watch, for ye know not when the time is; for, as a snare, death shall come on all them that dwell on the face of the whole earth.

41 When the Son of man shall come in his glory, and all the holy angels with him, then shall he sit on the throne of his glory.

42 And before him shall be gathered all na-

tions, and he shall separate them one from another as a shepherd divideth his sheep from the goats.

43 And he shall set the sheep on his right hand and the goats on his left hand.

44 Then shall the King say unto them on his right hand, Come, ye blessed of my Father, inherit the kingdom prepared for you from the foundation of the world.

45 For I was an hungered, and ye gave me meat; I was thirsty, and ye gave me drink; I was a stranger, and ye took me in, naked, and ye clothed me; I was sick, and ye visited me; I was in prison and ye came unto me.

46 Then shall the righteous answer him, saying, Lord, when saw we thee an hungered, and fed thee, or thirsty, and gave thee drink?

47 When saw we thee a stranger, and took thee in, or naked, and clothed thee?

48 Or when saw we thee sick or in prison, and came unto thee? And the King shall answer and say unto them, Verily I say unto you, Inasmuch as ye have done it to the least of my brethren, ye have done it unto me.

49 Then shall he say to them on his left hand Depart from me, ye cursed, into everlasting fire prepared for the devil and his angels.

50 For I was an hungered, and ye gave me no meat; I was thirsty, and ye gave me no drink; I was a stranger, and ye took me not in; naked, and ye clothed me not; sick and in prison, and ye visited me not.

51 Then they also answer, saying, Lord, when saw we thee an hungered, or athirst, or a stranger, or naked, or sick, or in prison, and did not minister unto thee?

52 Then shall He answer them, saying, Verily I say unto you, Inasmuch as ye did it not to one of the least of these, ye did it not unto me.

53 And these shall go away into everlasting punishment, but the righteous into life eternal.

54 And this gospel of the kingdom of God, and his righteousness, shall be preached in all the world, for a witness to all nations, so the world shall have no cloak for its sins.

55 Whosoever heareth these sayings of mine and doeth them, him will I liken unto a wise man, which built his house upon a rock.

56 And the rains descended, and the floods came, and the winds blew and beat vehemently on that house, and it fell not, for it was founded on a rock.

57 And whosoever heareth these sayings of mine and doeth them not, shall be likened unto a foolish man which built his house upon the sand.

58 And the rains descended, and the floods came, and the winds blew and beat upon that house, and great was the fall of it.

59 And it came to pass, when Jesus had ended these sayings, the people were astonished at his doctrines, for He spake as man never spake before, and taught them as one having authority.

60 And a certain scribe said unto Jesus, Master, I will follow thee wherever thou goest.

61 Jesus said unto him, The foxes have holes, and the birds have nests, but the Son of man hath not where to lay his head.

CHAPTER XII.

HEAVEN.

God created it and spread it out—Garnished it—He ruleth it—Many mansions—Each star a mansion—Full of angelic life—All good, clean, and beautiful—No marriages, pain, or sorrow there—Life is eternal—We will know each other—Angels travel and work—Work does not fatigue—All are young there—They are children of light, and they shine as the sun—They differ in glory, according to their works—Why we do not see them here—All are perfected there as their work shall be—God's voice fills the infinite heavens, cheering the angels—The mind cannot conceive the good things there—A star as bright as the morning star for the good—The sun and his planets our heaven—Nothing vile or unclean can enter heaven—The angels cannot get unclean—The raiment of the angels, peace and contentment.

1   The heavens declare the glory of God, and the firmament sheweth his power and wisdom.

2   Day unto day uttereth speech, and night unto night sheweth knowledge.

3   God created the heavens and the earth and spread them out by his light, his love, and his strength.

4   *And he called the firmament heaven*, and his speech and his law are perfect.

5   He has most beautifully garnished the heavens by his spirit and light.

6   Let the heavens rejoice and the earth be glad, for heaven is God's throne, and the earth is his footstool.

7   God ruleth the starry heavens by his light and his spirit, his love, his knowledge, and his strength.

8   He is greater than all and he fills the heavens and the earth, and he goes where and when he will

as an angel and as many great angels, and as all the angels and as all the gods. And in his house there are many mansions. Each star in the firmament is a mansion for him and his children, the angels.

9 Heaven is the house of God and is his throne, and is the abode of the angels, and is full of life, and is garnished so pure and clean that angels may love and worship God through eternity in their bright shining raiment and not soil or stain them, for they are the sons and daughters of God.

10 There is no dirt nor filth in heaven, nor moth nor rust. All is as clean as the light of the sun and as bright as the light of many suns.

11 The glory of God gives light to the heavens, and he hath wiped away all tears from all faces, and all sorrow from all hearts in heaven.

12 There is no death, nor pain, nor suffering; for all is peace, happiness, and joy.

13 There are no marriages in heaven as in this world; but the family circle and patriarchal groups prevail there, and every one is drawn to his father and mother and patriarchal group.

14 The angels of heaven know and rejoice with each other. There is no heat nor cold in heaven. Everything is the most beautiful, pleasant, and happy.

15 The feasts of heaven are always spread and the waters of life and the trees of life are abundant, but not like waters, trees, and feasts of this world; but are free to all, and conduce to eternal life, peace, and joy.

16 The heavens have no bounds, and life there is eternal. Ye cannot understand what eternity is, nor what infinity is, nor what God is, for he is both

infinity and eternity. Trouble not yourselves about these matters, but trust in God.

17 The angels can travel at will, but do not leave their own mansion or star till commanded to do so by their Father or his elect angels.

18 The angels work, and work does not fatigue them. Their chief work is to bring in young angels from this and like worlds, and to guide and comfort them, and teach them all truth, even in hell, if they are lost.

19 If a man or child dies in this world, they go for the young angel at once, and the angels of young children, dying in infancy, are nursed and reared up in heaven to be the most beautiful, perfect, and pleasant in the kingdom of God.

20 The angels sing hosannas and songs of praise to God, and music and dancing is heard in heaven. There is no music where their voices are not heard.

21 The angels are the comforters and guides of the dead. They keep the law and cheerfully obey God, Christ, the holy prophets, and the patriarchs.

22 They are the children of light, and shine forth as the sun in the kingdom of their Father.

23 Marvel not at this, for it is as easy for God to make an angel out of light as it is to make a man out of dust.

24 The body of man is weak, and will soon die; the body of the angel is strong, and will never die.

25 God is light, God is love, God is life, and is everlasting, and in him there is great strength; and by the strength of his life God made the infinite starry heavens and put them in motion, and keeps them in motion.

26 As God lives, they all must move as they do

now, and have always; for they are given action and indestructibility, as the angels are, by his life. All the suns, stars, and moons make obeisance to him, and in his life there is all strength and power.

27 In man there is life also, and that life exists in angel form in secret to him, and to all great physicians in this world. That life in man has made itself a habitation in this world, the natural body.

28 That life, or angel, within his natural body is not the product of the flesh of his body, but the body is the product of the soul within it. The soul gives the body life and action. It moves it about at its will.

29 The corporeal body of man may be destroyed by disease, by violence, or worn out by old age, when it is no longer fit for the soul to inhabit, and will no longer work at the will of the soul.

30 The soul then withdraws gently through the brain and eyes, and is received by its kindred angels and is taken to heaven. The body when thus left is but a carcass, and is never more needed by the soul, and it returns to dust.

31 The human eye is the organ that denotes the soul of an angel that is within man.

32 God is perfect; his law is perfect. Man is not perfect, but he is feeble. Still he is progressing through this world, and as sure as law prevails, he will soon find himself in heaven, there to be rewarded a thousand fold for every good deed and thought rendered in this world.

33 This is true, even if the wicked are drawn through hell for repentance, preparation, and instruction, and remain there till rendered worthy of heaven.

34 Our Father in heaven is light and life, and

he is God of all the gods, and is as a consuming fire in his love and goodness.

35 Our Mother in heaven is love, and she is the goddess of heaven, and the most beautiful, kind, merciful, and good of all.

36 Truth and mercy are her handmaids.

37 Truth is the judge of the people of this world and of all nations, and she holds justice in her right hand.

38 Mercy gives to each angel its reward, most bounteously awarded by truth, and holds alms and charity in her right hand.

39 Christ, our Lord and Master, is Lord of lords, and King of kings, and a great teacher of the holy word of God, and is an angel elect.

40 These five agree as one.

41 The man's body is made of earth. The angel's body is made of light, and will not perish, but will live for evermore.

42 As one star differeth from another in glory in the starry heavens, so do the angels of the resurrection in heaven. In heaven there are the least angels and great angels, and perfect or mighty angels, and great elect angels.

43 There is also life, and life more abundant, and perfect life, which have been determined by the angel's sins in this life, and by the man himself while here on earth.

44 This difference of angels in the kingdom of heaven is as thirty is to one hundred, and all the way between these numbers.

45 For the wicked sinners, even murderers, have more good works than they are usually credited with in this world, and every good work shall have its reward.

46 The least angels have all the happiness and joy in heaven they can contain, on the principle that the child in its mother's arms is as happy as its mother.

47 Marvel not, nor doubt not, because ye can not see the angels of heaven. A man, before he is born into this world, has eyes, and cannot see; he has ears, and cannot hear the things of this world; but when he is born and awakened into the world, he sees and hears them.

48 He can also dimly and faintly see and hear the things of heaven. He is almost blind and deaf as to heaven, but the veil of secrecy is sometimes lifted away.

49 When he dies in the flesh, he is born again; he is then born an angel in heaven unto eternal life, and then he sees and hears perfectly. He sees the angels and hears them perfectly.

50 He sees the things of the Father and is taught of the Father by the angels. The angels of heaven can only see of the Father, he is so great.

51 God, our Father in heaven, is greater than all. He fills the heavens and the earth with his Spirit, and his light, and his life. His love, his mercy, his strength, his knowledge, his perception, his waters of life, and feasts, and his goodness abound all through the heavens forever.

52 He seeth and heareth all things. He is not far away, but is a God at hand.

53 His voice fills the infinite heavens, enlivening the angels and cheering them, and commanding men to keep his holy commandments and not do evil, and love and trust in him. This voice of God speaking to man *is conscience*.

54 In heaven the angels are all young in ap-

pearance. Adam and Eve are young. The old patriarchs, prophets, the old grandmothers and grandfathers are all young angels, and though perfected in heaven, yet are as readily known by their children as when they were here in this world.

55 There are no gray hairs or wrinkles there, but all are perfect as their works are. The old are made young, and every girl has her best boy, and every boy has his best girl. And the weak are made strong, and the wicked made good and humble and obedient, but are not very great, because of their evil deeds.

56 God's children rejoice in his love and majesty, and will not worship each other, nor any but him.

57 Nothing that is vile, unclean, or wicked can enter heaven.

58 Bow, all ye men, women, and children. Bow, all ye nations of the earth, and render obedience unto God.

59 For eye hath not seen, ear hath not heard, neither can the mind of man conceive the good things that God hath prepared for them who love him and keep his commandments to the best of their ability and their opportunities.

60 God and the angels have senses and powers that can not be understood in this world, and pleasures and joys unknown to us.

61 Seek ye the kingdom of God and his love and righteousness, and all these things shall be added unto you.

62 And ye shall appear in the glory of your Father in heaven as his sons and daughters.

63 Come out from the tombs of unbelief, of idolatry and wickedness, and love and worship God

and keep his commandments, lest ye fall short of his glory he has provided for you.

64 Every star in the starry heavens is one of the mansions that God has made for his children, and is suited to the tastes and the pleasures of all of them. Heaven has room for all, and is the resting-place for all the people of God.

65 The stars of heaven are clean and pure, and of the finest and most durable material, and of the finest architecture. They are very beautiful, and many of them enchantingly so, and so as to suit the tastes and pleasures of all the angels in heaven, however great or small the angel may be.

66 The wedding garments or raiment of the angels are not made with hands, but they arise from the glory and strength of their bodies.

67 And their crowns of glory, on their heads, that fade not away, are not made with hands, but arise from the love, humility, wisdom, and intelligence of the angel.

68 The raiment and the crowns of glory are perfectly satisfactory and pleasing to each angel in heaven, for they are all splendid and charming to each, and all that is required to fill the measure of joy of each and every one.

69 All are satisfied and pleased with their rewards, and love, plenty, and peace reign in heaven, and all the angels rejoice in their glory, and love and praise God.

70 Thy heaven is dimly in thy sight. Fear not, and doubt not, for your Father in heaven is your friend, and will finally draw all of you into heaven, and gather you unto your fathers and mothers.

71 For the heavens are many and great, and

God is greater than all the heavens, but his children the elect angels assist in the government of heaven;

72 But have no power to change the laws of God, for that would shake the heavens.

73 The wicked are not great in heaven, but the good and obedient are great.

74 The elect angels are gods and goddesses, and abound throughout the infinite and eternal heavens.

75 That great luminary, our sun, and his system of planets around his power and subject to him and committed to his care, is our heaven and is our home, where we shall live for ever and for ever.

76 Christ said, And unto him that is faithful unto the end will I give the morning star.

77 And he said, I am the bright and morning star.

CHAPTER XIII.

HELL AND THE EXILE.

Hell is a purgatory to remove sins—A school of instruction and repentance and cleansing—Sinners cleansed by God's love and righteousness, not by fire—The work is done by angels—Hell is the sinner's condition—First, second, and third divisions of hell—Repentance in hell—Finally each arises and goes to God, as they repent, until they all go—Necessity for a hell—God's love for sinners the same as a mother's love for her child—The land and the sea—Death and hell must give up their dead unto God—The angel of hell is his servant—The blight of sin after repentance—Falling short of the glory of God is eternal punishment.

1 Hell is a purgatory for the removal of the scales and stains of sin from the wicked, and reforming of unworthy sinners; but it cannot remove the blight and abasement that sinners bring on themselves by voluntary and uncalled-for sins committed in the service of mammon and Satan.

2 It is the only preparatory school for the wicked of this world. There they are purified and taught, so as to be worthy of heaven; and without which they cannot enter the kingdom of heaven.

3 When a sinner is so vile that he is not worthy to enter heaven, he is lost in hell; and that is his only refuge and is his choice, and he readily goes there.

4 Heaven is God's throne, and this earth is his footstool, and hell is an advancement over this world. *Hell is not hot nor cold.*

5 It is the sinner's condition that troubles him. His weakness in mind and body is his ailment.

6 The abasement and blight of his sins seem to him as fire in hell, but it is not. The separation

of sin or evil from the good in the angel shows up the weakness and folly of both mind and body of each transgressor of God's holy laws.

7 The sun of God's love and righteousness and truth shines down upon the sinner in hell with cleansing and purifying in its light and wings.

8 In course of time it separates the evil from the good in the lost sinner, and each sinner in hell, as a shepherd divideth his goats from his sheep, and as the harvester divideth the tares from the wheat.

9 The tares, or evil portion of the sinner, are burned, as it were; but the good portion of him is saved in heaven, let that be great or small, and constitutes the life and measure of the angel.

10 This must be done, and the sinner made pure and righteous before he can be admitted into heaven, for nothing impure can enter there.

11 And when released from hell and admitted into heaven, no power there can change the reward and measure of joy of that angel; for it is then full, according to its works.

12 The law has fixed its measure, in body and mind, according to its works, and it must remain so; and in that respect punishment is eternal, but is not done of God, but of the sinner himself.

13 The sinner may make proportional advancement with the righteous in heaven, but never so much as to break his rank and measure of rewards in heaven. As the tree falleth, so it lieth, in rank and rewards.

14 . Hell has no dominion or power over the good and righteous. The angels of heaven may visit it with safety and with pleasure. With joy they see it is for the best, and that the fallen and lost angels are making rapid progress.

15   All that is vile and mean in man is drawn from his soul in hell; and when the soul of man is thus purified, as if by fire, it is not yet prepared for heaven.

16   It must hear the gospel of love, righteousness, mercy, humility, justice, and charity, and must believe it, repent, and remember their Father in heaven.

17   Then they can arise and go to their Father in heaven and receive the same royal welcome in like manner that the prodigal son received, and be rewarded for all the good works or fruits they bear.

18   This preparation in hell is accomplished by the most competent teachers sent from heaven; for God will not entrust the care of his children in hell to any other.

19   The chief angel of hell is a great teacher and doctor of divinity, and is a great angel and servant of God. So are all of his angels who assist him, male and female.

20   They do their work so thoroughly that all unbelief, hypocrisy, whitewashing, cloaks for sin, lying, greed, covetousness, false teaching, pride, and evil will disappear like a heavy frost before a summer's sun, and never to return again on that angel.

21   Our Lord and Master, Jesus Christ, left the right hand of the power of God, and went and preached to the spirits of the lost in the prison of hell; and the angels teach in turn, only not always the same ones.

22   When fully prepared, each one receives the wedding garment or raiment and crown of glory, foolish virgins and all, according to their respective merits; and they arise and are conducted to paradise in heaven, and are received with joy and

shouts of their brethren and sisters and their Father.

23 This ye call the damnation of hell, but is the salvation of God unto the wicked.

24 There are three grades of hell. The first is for the very wicked, such as murderers, robbers, oppressors of the poor and weak, blasphemers against the Holy Ghost.

25 Some of these remain in hell a thousand years before they repent.

26 The second grade of hell is for lesser transgressors. In it are those who will not work for their living when able; are beaten with stripes (as it were) to reform them; and so with many other sinners of lesser grades of sins.

27 The third grade is for those who are guilty of the least sins, and is for prodigals, spendthrifts, blackguards, and such like.

28 Each heaven in the infinite starry firmament has a hell unto itself, for there are many worlds of men like this, and nothing vile or unclean can enter into our heaven, or any heaven in God's infinite creation, or all would be strife and confusion, and there would be no rest, joy, or pleasure in the whole heavens.

29 What greater love hath any than a mother has for her child, except God? Yet in its infancy and helplessness, and when able to crawl, and it gets filthy, she will prepare herself and take it in her lap and wash it clean, put on clean clothes, comb its hair, and nurse it, and then put it to bed, greatly improved and benefited by her care and labor.

30 But while she is doing this, her infant child will cry and kick. As her infant boy grows larger, she will sometimes chastise him with stripes, if her persuasion will not suffice to make him obedient.

31 She teaches him till he is prepared to enter upon the duties of life in this world.

32 Who will say she does not love her child, or that she rears him up into manhood through malice, hatred, or revenge to her child?

33 Nay, she does these humble services to her infant boy through the most tender love, mercy, goodness, and hope for her boy.

34 And God doth the like unto all of his children at all times, at all places, and in all conditions.

35 He chastens, as a mother, whom he loveth, and does the best he can for all. Trust in him, for he loves you, and his tender mercy endureth forever unto all.

36 *For the sea and the land, and death and hell, shall give up their dead unto him,* and all shall be rewarded for their good works in glory.

37 And they must be given up to him immediately they die in this world, and receive their rewards in heaven, if just and righteous in heart; if not, for his preparation, reform, and instruction in hell. For no man, woman, or child ever was in a grave, unless buried alive, but only his carcass, and that profiteth nothing evermore; for who would exchange his heavenly body of beauty, of strength, of power, of glory, and of life everlasting for a body of clay, dust, and death?

38 This is the only use or need of hell. But the abasement and blight of the soul, and his capacity for honor, pleasure, and joy in heaven, can never be changed in earth, hell, or heaven, except by good works here on earth.

39 The angels that sin are cast down to hell and are lost by their sins, and are reserved unto repentance and unto a second judgment, which

occurs when they are able to pass that judgment and go to the Father.

40 A man's mother would not seek to take her son out of hell and introduce him into heaven until he was made worthy and truly prepared, for there is no cloak to sin in heaven.

41 But the wicked man should forsake his ways, and the unrighteous man his thoughts, and turn unto God and his love and righteousness, here in this world, and escape the damnation of hell and his loss of glory in the kingdom of God.

42 Fear sin, the devil, and hell, for it is everlasting loss to your souls; and this loss of glory is represented by such words as "everlasting punishment," "hell-fire," "damnation," "shall perish," "bottomless pit," and "destruction," because the soul cannot recover from it, even in heaven.

THE EXILE.

Its nature—A matter of choice for some angels—Only the very wicked choose it—Blasphemy against the Holy Ghost—Such choose the exile—If a man is punished in this world, he will not be in the next—Angels in exile have all the feasts of heaven, and are contented.

1 There are crimes committed by men, though they repent in hell and are purified, and go to their Father in heaven and receive all the rewards and joy they can contain, yet the glory of God and heaven is too great and splendid for them.

2 And they shall choose a place in heaven which is less resplendent. The glory of heaven around the throne of God is more than they wish, and they separate themselves and are assigned to a place less splendid, so as to suit them, and this place is the exile.

3 Such sinners committed blasphemy against

the Holy Ghost by killing their fellow-man, or by human oppression in its many forms, in this world, without cause.

4 Their shame and degradation is less visible in the exile, and they choose it and go there voluntarily.

5 If, however, a man killeth another man in this world and is tried and convicted of murder, and pays the penalty with his life, and confesses the crime and asks pardon of God and man, that is a full atonement here and in heaven.

6 And if he steals and confesses his crime on the cross, as the thief did, and asks to be pardoned, that is a full atonement in earth and heaven.

7 These angels in exile have all the joy they can contain, and the tree of life and the waters of life and feasts of heaven in abundance and freely, but they cannot endure the best places in heaven. It is more than they like, and they go into exile as a matter of pleasure and choice, where they can better enjoy themselves in their conditions.

8 For heaven is beautifully variegated, so as to suit the tastes, joys, and pleasures of the angels, whatever their conditions may be.

9 The good and righteous shun the exile, for it is not suited to them and their tastes and pleasures.

10 Let all shun it and live nearer to the throne of God.

CHAPTER XIV.

Christ's ministry—He sends out his disciples to preach—They return with joy—Jesus baptized not, but his disciples—He goes to the Feast of Tabernacles and preaches—Warned that Herod would kill him—Great multitudes hear him preach—The transfiguration of Christ to angel form—His glorious appearance—What he did during his ministry—He ordains his church—Gives St. Peter, his oldest apostle, the keys to heaven—Jesus and his disciples go to Jerusalem at the Feast of the Passover—They went by Jacob's Well to Bethany—There a supper was given them—Mary, the sister of Martha, anoints his head and feet against his death and burial—His triumphal entry into Jerusalem—He drove the money-changers from the temple with a scourge of small plaited ropes—He and his apostles eat the Passover—He instituted the sacrament of his supper—Washes his disciples' feet—He appoints Judas, and commanded him to betray him, and ordered him to do so quickly—Poor Judas humbly obeys his Master, and then hanged himself for grief.

1 Jesus preached this gospel of the kingdom of God, on the mount, on the plains, on the sea, in the temple and synagogue at Jerusalem, and throughout all Jewry.

2 Jesus sent his twelve disciples out to preach the gospel of the kingdom of God.

3 And then he sent seventy more in couples, saying unto them, Preach that the Kingdom of God is nigh unto you.

4 This was during his ministry. The disciples returned with joy at their success.

5 And Jesus said, I beheld Satan as lightning fall from heaven.

6 Jesus made and baptized more disciples than John;

7 Though Jesus baptized not, but his disciples.

8 Jesus went up to Jerusalem at the Feast of

Tabernacles, and taught in the temple in the daytime, and went out to the Mount of Olives at night, though he was warned that Herod would kill him.

9 And great multitudes followed him and came to hear him preach. The Jews laid no hand on him.

10 Jesus took part of his disciples out into a high mountain, and was transfigured before them, and his face did shine as the sun, and his raiment was white as the light.

11 And behold, there appeared Moses and Elijah talking with him. A bright cloud overshadowed them, and a voice came out of the cloud, saying:

12 This is my beloved Son, in whom I am well pleased; hear ye him. And the disciples were sore afraid.

13 Jesus, during his ministry, healed the sick, made the lame whole, cast out devils or evil spirits, opened the eyes of the blind, fed the hungry, raised the dead, walked on the sea, stilled the tempest, and preached the gospel to the poor.

14 When Jesus came into the coasts of Philippi he asked his disciples, Whom do men say I am?

15 And they said, Some say thou art John the Baptist risen from the dead; some say thou art Elijah the prophet, or one of the old prophets.

16 And he said unto them, Whom do ye say that I am?

17 Then Peter answered, saying, Thou art the Christ, the Son of the living God.

18 And Jesus answered, Blessed art thou, Peter; for flesh and blood hath not revealed this unto thee, but my Father in heaven.

19 On this rock will I build my church; and the gates of hell shall not prevail against it.

20 And I will give unto thee the keys of the kingdom of heaven; and whatsoever ye shall justly bind on earth shall be bound in heaven, and whatsoever ye loose on earth shall be loosed in heaven.

21 And from that time Jesus began to show unto his disciples how he must go into Jerusalem and suffer many things of the chief priests, elders, and scribes, and be killed, and rise again on the third day.

22 Then Peter said, Far be it from thee, Lord; this thing shall not come unto thee.

23 Then Jesus said, Get thee behind me, Satan; thou savorest too much of the things of this world, and not the things of God.

24 Then Jesus and his disciples returned into Galilee, and in the thirty-third year of his age, the Feast of the Passover drew nigh.

25 And Jesus took his twelve apostles to him, and said, We go up to Jerusalem, and there shall the Son of man be delivered to the Gentiles and be crucified, and shall rise again on the third day.

26 Then Jesus began his journey to Jerusalem to preach and celebrate the Passover, and a great multitude of men and women followed him.

27 Then Jesus and his disciples came to Jericho, and there he healed Zaccheus, the publican, and from thence they journeyed on to Jerusalem, going by Jacob's Well.

28 They arrived at Bethany, a small town about three miles from Jerusalem, six days before the Feast of the Passover;

29 Where they made him a supper, and Martha served.

30 Then took Mary, the sister of Lazarus, whom Jesus had raised from the dead, a pound of

very costly ointment and anointed Jesus, and wiped his feet with her hair, against his death and burial.

31 Then Jesus said, Verily I say unto you, Wheresoever this gospel shall be preached in the whole world, this also shall be spoken of, for a memorial of her.

32 From Bethany Jesus and his disciples made a most triumphal entry into Jerusalem. Many of his disciples came out to meet him.

33 And many spread their garments in the way, and many cut down branches off the trees and strewed them in the way.

34 And the multitude cried, Hosannah! Blessed is he that cometh in the name of the Lord. Hosannah in the highest!

35 And when Jesus was come into Jerusalem, all the city was moved, saying, Who is this?

36 And the multitude said, This is Jesus, the prophet of Nazareth of Galilee.

37 And Jesus went into the temple of God, and cast out all of them that sold and bought in the temple, and overthrew the tables of the money-changers, and scourged them out of the temple with a scourge of small plaited ropes.

38 And said unto them, It is written, *My house shall be called a house of prayer; but ye have made it a den of thieves.*

39 And the blind and lame came to him in the temple, and he healed them. And when the chief priest, elders, and scribes saw the wonderful things he did, and the children crying in the temple, Hosannah to the son of David! they were sore displeased and took counsel to kill him.

40 He left the temple in the evening, and

41 In the morning he came back to the temple and taught in it, and again healed the sick, the lame and blind, and continued to preach the gospel of the kingdom of God and heal the sick till Thursday evening.

42 He well knew that the priests and elders had conspired to take him and put him to death on the cross.

43 In the daytime he was teaching in the temple, and at night he went out and abode in the Mount of Olives, and the people came early in the morning to hear him.

44 Now the Passover drew nigh, and the chief priests and scribes sought how they might kill him; for they feared the people.

45 On Wednesday certain Pharisees and scribes came to Jesus, saying, Get thee out, and depart hence, for Herod will kill thee.

46 And Jesus said unto them, Go ye and tell him that I preach the gospel in the temple and cast out devils, and I do cures to-day and to-morrow, and on the third day (meaning Friday) *I shall be perfected* (meaning through death).

47 It cannot be possible that a prophet shall perish out of Jerusalem.

48 Then Jesus sent Peter and John, saying, Go and prepare us the Passover, that we may eat.

49 And they went and made ready the Passover; and when the hour was come, he sat down with the twelve apostles.

50 And he said unto them, I have desired to eat this Passover with you before I suffer;

51 For I will not eat any more with you, till it be fulfilled in the kingdom of God.

52 And as they were eating, Jesus took bread, and blessed it, and brake it, and gave it to the disciples, and said, Take, eat; this is my body.

53 And he took the cup, and gave thanks, and gave it to them, saying, Drink ye all of it;

54 For this is my blood of the new testament, which is shed for many for the remission of sins.

55 But I say unto you, I will not drink henceforth of this fruit of the vine, until that day when I drink it new with you in my Father's kingdom.

56 Truly the Son of man goeth as it was determined; and behold, and the hand of him that shall betray me is with me on the table.

57 And they began to be sorrowful, and to inquire among themselves which of them it was that should do this thing. And they began to ask Jesus, Lord, is it I? Lord, is it I?

58 Then Jesus said, I speak not of all of you: I know whom I have chosen: but that the scripture may be fulfilled, He that eateth bread with me shall lift up his heel against me.

59 Then Jesus, when he had thus said, he was troubled, and said unto them, Verily I say unto you, that one of you shall betray me.

60 Then the disciples looked one on another, doubting of whom he spake.

61 John was lying on Jesus' breast, and Peter beckoned him that he ask Jesus who it should be.

62 John then asked, Lord, who is it?

63 And Jesus answered, He it is to whom I shall give a sop.

64 And when he dipped the sop, he gave it to Judas Iscariot, the son of Simon.

65 And then said Jesus to Judas, *That thou doest, do quickly.*

66 Judas, being thus selected to act in the great tragedy of his Master's death, went out in the night immediately.

67 Then said Jesus, Now is the Son of man glorified, and God is glorified in him.

68 Then Jesus riseth from supper, and took a towel and girded it about him, and after that he poured water into a basin and washed his disciples' feet, teaching them love, humility, and charity.

69 Then Judas went, in pursuance of the commission of his Master, and saw the chief priests and elders, and they gave him thirty pieces of silver to betray Jesus into their hands.

70 Judas was treasurer of Christ's church, and was not aware that the Jews could take or destroy his Master.

71 Then Jesus and his disciples sang a hymn and departed, and went out to the Mount of Olives, where he preached his farewell sermon to his disciples.

72 This was on Thursday evening before our present Easter Sunday, and in the thirty-third year of his age.

CHAPTER XV.

Christ's farewell to his disciples—He cried and said, "I and my Father are one, but he is greater than I; he is greater than all"—All things made known to the disciples—He sends them to preach—Love and peace enjoined—Life in heaven—He to be cast out from this earth—"Be not troubled"—Ye shall live—He will draw all men unto him—The Holy Spirit of truth—False prophets—"Judge ye what is right, but err not"—Christ is the way—Follow him—God judges no man, nor Christ, but the law—Christ came from the Father and goeth again to him—"In our Father's house are many mansions"—Be not afraid, but cheerful in your tribulations—He promises to come again—His prayer for the world and disciples.

1 Jesus cried and said, He that believeth on me believeth not on me, but on him that sent me; and he that seeth me seeth him that sent me.

2 I and my Father are one, but my Father is greater than I; he is greater than all. He fills the heavens and the earth with his light, spirit, love, perception, and goodness.

3 I have not spoken of myself, but the Father which sent me gave me a commandment what I should say, and what I should speak, and I know his commandment is life everlasting.

4 Even as the Father said unto me, so I speak and do.

5 *All things that I have heard of the Father I have made known to you;* and as I was sent by him to preach the gospel of the kingdom of God, his truth, his love, mercy, charity, and righteousness, so I send you to preach it unto the world.

6 And ye shall impose no burden on my disciples, except to abstain from idols and from sacrifices and burnt offerings, and keep my commandments

7 I am the true vine and our Father is the husbandman. I am the vine and ye are branches.

8 He that abideth in me shall bring forth much fruit, and herein our Father is glorified, that ye bring much fruit, or good works.

9 But without me and my gospel ye can do nothing.

10 Remember, there is the least and the great in the kingdom of heaven.

11 And there is life, and there is life more abundant, and there is perfect life of the elect, according to the good fruits ye bear.

12 And there is damnation, and there is damnation the greater, and there is the damnation of hell, according to the evil fruits ye bear.

13 If ye abide in me and my commandments, ye shall ask what ye will, and it shall be done unto you.

14 As the Father loveth me, so I love you. Continue ye in my love.

15 This is my commandment of the Father, that ye love one another, as I have loved you.

16 If ye keep my commandments, ye shall abide in my love, even as I have kept our Father's commandments and abide in his love; and he that shall not try to keep his commandments does not love or believe in him.

17 If ye love me, keep my commandments; if ye ask anything in my name, I will do it.

18 If any man serve me, let him follow me; and where I am, there shall my servant be.

19 And if any man serve me, him will our Father honor.

20 Now is the judgment of this world; now shall the prince of this world be cast out.

21 *And I, when I be lifted up, will draw all men unto me.*

22 Then Jesus said unto them, Yet a little while is the light with you; while ye have the light believe in the light, that ye may be the children of light.

23 Let not your hearts be troubled. Ye that believe in God, believe in me also, and believe me that I am in the Father, and the Father in me.

24 My Father doeth the works.

25 Yet a little while and the world seeth me no more; but ye shall see me, because I go unto my Father.

26 And because I live, ye shall live also in the kingdom of heaven; and he that loveth me shall be loved of my Father, and I will love him and manifest myself unto him.

27 In that day ye shall see me as I am.

28 It is expedient that I go away, for then I will send you the Comforter, which is the Holy Ghost, and he will reprove the world of sin, of righteousness, and of judgment.

29 And when the Spirit of truth comes, he will guide you unto all truth.

30 He will show you things to come, and he shall receive of mine, and show you thine kindred and brethren. All things the Father hath are mine, and all shall be thine if ye continue in my words.

31 Beware of false prophets and false teachers.

32 Ye shall know them by their fruits. If the blind lead the blind, shall they not both fall into the ditch?

33 Do men gather grapes of thorns, or figs of thistles?

34 Even so, every good tree bringeth forth

good fruit, but a corrupt tree bringeth forth evil fruit.

35 God hath given thee life, and hath also given thee reason, and hath commanded all men to exercise and improve that reason; and yea, why even of yourselves judge ye not what is right, and what is good, and what is evil? But do not err.

36 If any man shall come after me and shall teach the commandments of God, and keep them, then he is indeed my disciple.

37 But if he teaches the doctrines, the traditions, the superstitions and follies of men, follow him not.

38 FOLLOW THOU ME.

39 *I am the way, the truth, the resurrection, and the life.*

40 Remember the word I said unto you, The servant is not greater than his master, nor the disciple greater than his lord. Follow my commandments.

41 Little children, yet a little while and ye shall see me no more. Now I go my way to him that sent me.

42 My kingdom is not of this world. He that loveth me loveth the Father also, and he that hateth me hateth the Father also.

43 God judgeth no man; neither do I. If any man heareth my words, and believeth them not, I judge him not, *for I came not to judge, but to save the world.*

44 But he that rejecteth me, and keepeth not my words, hath one that judgeth him.

45 *The word of truth that I have spoken shall judge him in the last day.*

46 Again a little while and ye shall see me,

because I go to the Father in heaven, and there ye shall come also.

47 Verily, I say unto you, Ye shall weep and lament, and ye shall be sorrowful, but your sorrow shall there be turned into joy.

48 I will see you again and your heart shall rejoice, and your joy no man taketh away from you.

49 Verily, I say unto you, Whatsoever ye ask the Father in my name, he will give it to you.

50 *I need not pray the Father, for he loveth you, and in that day will give you whatsoever ye ask of him.*

51 And to whom much is given, much is required; and to whom little is given, little is required.

52 Ask and ye shall receive, that the measure of your joy shall be full.

53 What shall the measure of thy joy be?

54 These things have I spoken unto you, proverbs and parables, but the time cometh when I shall no more speak to you in proverbs.

55 But I will show you plainly of the Father, and the Spirit of truth shall guide you into all truth, and shall teach you all things, and shall bring all things to your remembrance, even all things I have said unto you.

56 I came forth from the Father into this world, and now I leave the world and go again to the Father.

57 Let not your hearts be troubled:

58 In my Father's house there are many mansions: if it were not so, I would not tell you so. And I go to prepare a place for you.

59 And when I go and prepare a place for you, I will come again and receive you unto myself, that where I am ye may be also.

60 And whither I go ye know, and ye know the way.

61 There the blessings and glory of God shall surpass the knowledge of mortal man.

62 I will not leave you comfortless. I will pray the Father, and he will give you another Comforter, that shall abide with you forever; even the Spirit of truth, whom the world cannot receive.

63 Peace I give unto you, my peace I leave with you: not as the world giveth, give I unto you.

64 Let not thy heart be troubled, neither let it be afraid.

65 I go away, and again I shall come unto you and receive you to myself.

66 In the world ye shall have your tribulations, but we shall all meet again in heaven, where God shall wipe away all tears from all eyes, and all sorrow from all hearts.

67 Be patient and of good cheer, for I have overcome the world.

CHRIST'S PRAYER.

68 Then Jesus lifted up his eyes to heaven and said, Father, the hour is come; glorify thy Son, that thy Son may glorify thee.

69 I have glorified thee on earth: *I have finished the work thou gavest me to do.*

70 And now glorify me, O Father, with thine own glory which I had with thee before the world was.

71 I have manifested thy name to the people of this world that thou gavest me.

72 I have given unto them the words thou gavest me, and as I was sent into this world to preach

the gospel and make thy will known, so I have sent my disciples.

73 Now I come unto thee, and as I have glorified thee on earth, glorify me in heaven.

74 Of all thou gavest me in this world, I have lost none except Satan, the son of perdition.

75 I pray for my disciples, and for all the people of this earth, which are here in this world, and for all who may come after them in thy holy name.

76 Father, I will that where I am they may be also.

77 Sanctify them through thy truth.

78 THY WORD IS TRUTH.

79 And thine shall be the kingdon, and the power, and the glory, for ever. Amen.

CHAPTER XVI.

Christ would not flee—His agony in the garden—Hi[s]
arrest—Peter cut off one of Malchus's ears—Christ healed it—
He that taketh the sword shall perish by the sword—Pete[r]
denied Christ—Jesus was taken before the high priest—H[e]
avowed that he was Christ—Had spoken nothing in secret—A[n]
officer strikes Jesus—Crowing of the cock—Peter wept—Jesu[s]
taken before Pilate for trial—Judas was so grieved that h[e]
hanged himself—Jesus was tried first before Pilate, wh[o]
acquitted him—On a demand by the priests, he was sent be
fore Herod, who acquitted him—Pilate acquitted him agaim—
But, for fear of Cæsar, Pilate delivered Jesus to be crucified—
His crucifixion—His resurrection—On the cross he forgive
his slayers—Committed his mother to John's care—At hi[s]
death angels appear—Also at his resurrection and ascension.

1 When Jesus ended his farewell to his disci[-]
ples, he was yet at liberty, and if he had so desired
he might have escaped out of Judea, in any direction

2 But he led his disciples from Mount Olive[t]
down to the brook Cedron near by Jerusalem, an[d]
there they entered into a garden called Gethsem
ane, as they were wont to do.

3 Then Jesus saith unto them, All ye shall b[e]
offended because of me this night, for the shepher[d]
shall be smitten and the flock shall be scattered.

4 But Peter answered, Though all men shal[l]
be offended, I will not.

5 Jesus said unto him, Verily I say unto thee[,]
This night, before the cock crow twice, thou shal[l]
deny me thrice. Peter said, I will die with thee an[d]
not deny thee, and so said all his disciples.

6 Jesus said, Now is my soul troubled. Wha[t]
shall I say? shall I say, Father, save me from thi[s]
hour? But for this cause, came I unto this hour.

7 Father, glorify thy name. Then came [a]

voice from heaven, saying, I have glorified it, and will glorify it again.

8 The people said it thundered; others said an angel spoke. Jesus said, This voice came not for my sake, but your sakes.

9 Then Jesus said to his disciples, Sit ye here till I go and pray. And he took some of his disciples, and he prayed, saying:

10 O my Father, if it be possible, let this cup pass from me: nevertheless, *thy will be done, and not mine.*

11 Then he came to his disciples, and found them heavy with sleep. He went away the second time and prayed, saying, Father, if this cup may not pass away from me except I drink it, Thy will be done. And he prayed the third time, saying the same.

12 And Christ was in an agony when he prayed, and his sweat was, as it were, great drops of blood falling down to the ground. And there appeared an angel unto him from heaven, strengthening him. (Luke xxii. 43.) When he arose from prayer, he found his disciples asleep.

13 And he said unto them, Rise. And behold a multitude came out from Jerusalem, sent by the chief priests and elders, with swords and staves, to take Jesus, and they were led by Judas, who betrayed him with a kiss.

14 Jesus said unto them, Whom seek ye? and they said, Jesus of Nazareth. Jesus then said unto them, *I am he.*

15 Then they went backward and fell to the ground. Then Jesus said again, Whom seek ye? and they said, Jesus of Nazareth.

16 Jesus saith, I told ye I am he: therefore if ye seek me, let these my disciples go their way.

17 Then Peter drew his sword and he smote the high priest's servant and cut off his right ear. That servant's name was Malchus.

18 Then Jesus said unto Peter, Put up thy sword, for all that taketh the sword shall perish by the sword, and the cup which my Father hath given me, shall I not drink it? Jesus then touched the ear of Malchus, and it was healed.

19 He then, voluntarily, surrendered his body to the chief priests and elders.

20 Then the band and captain and officers of the Jews took Jesus and bound him.

21 Then Jesus said unto the chief priests, elders and captain of the temple which came unto him.

22 Be ye come out as against a thief, with swords and staves? I was daily in the temple teaching, and ye laid no hand on me.

23 Then they led him away to Annas first, and then to Caiaphas, who was high priest that year and the son-in-law of Annas.

24 His disciple John followed and went into the priest's palace with Jesus, for he was acquainted with him. And Peter followed and stood without the door.

25 Then John spake to her that kept the door, and brought Peter in.

26 Then she said unto Peter, Art thou not also one of this man's disciples? And Peter saith, I am not.

27 The high priest then asked Jesus of his disciples and doctrines. And Jesus answered him, saying,

28 I spake openly to the world; I ever taught in the temple and synagogue, whither the Jews always resort; *and in secret have I said nothing.*

29 They know my doctrines; ask them. Then one of the officers struck Jesus on the face. Jesus said unto him, If I have spoken evil, bear witness of it; but if well, why smitest thou me?

30 Peter stood and warmed himself, and they said to him, Art thou not one of his disciples? Peter again denied it.

31 Then cometh one of the maids of the high priest and said unto Peter, Thou art surely one of his disciples, and Peter, with an oath, denied his Master.

32 Then the cock crew, and Peter remembered his Master's words, and went out and wept.

33 This was about 2 o'clock Friday morning in April, A. D. 33 of Christ's birth.

34 Then the chief priests and elders and all the Jewish council sought false witnesses against Jesus to put him to death, but found none, but many came. At length two came, but their witness did not agree.

35 They sought witnesses from Galilee, his own country, but found none.

36 Then the high priest questioned Jesus again, but he held his peace.

37 Then the high priest said unto Jesus, I adjure thee by the living God, tell us whether thou be the Christ, the Son of the living God.

38 Then Jesus said, *I am. And ye shall see me sitting on the right hand of the power of God, and of glory.*

39 Then the high priest rent his clothes, saying, What need have we of more witnesses? He hath spoken blasphemy.

40 And they say, He is guilty of death. And then spit on Jesus and beat him.

41 When the morning was come, all the chief priests and the elders took counsel against Jesus to put him to death.

42 They said, Behold, the world has gone after him. And when they had bound him, they led him to Pilate, the governor, for trial.

43 Then Judas Iscariot repented, when he saw the reality of his Master's situation, and he brought back the thirty pieces of silver to the chief priests and elders, saying, I have betrayed innocent blood.

44 And they said unto him, What is that to us? See thou to that.

45 And he cast down the thirty pieces of silver in the temple, and was so overwhelmed with sorrow and grief that he went out and hanged himself.

46 Pilate entered the judgment hall, and the chief priests and elders and multitude began to accuse Jesus, saying, We found this fellow perverting the nation and forbidding to give tribute to Cæsar, and saying himself is Christ, a king.

47 Pilate asked Jesus if he was a king. Jesus said unto him, My kingdom is not of this world.

48 Pilate said to the chief priests and the people, I find no fault in him.

49 They were the more fierce, saying, He stirs up the people throughout all Jewry, beginning at Cana in Galilee.

50 When Pilate heard that Jesus was a Galilean, he sent him to Herod, the tetrarch of Galilee, because he belonged to Herod's jurisdiction.

51 But Herod had come to Jerusalem, and they immediately carried Jesus before Herod for trial.

52 Herod was exceedingly glad when he saw Jesus, for he hoped to see him perform a miracle.

53 He questioned him with many words; the chief priests and scribes stood by and accused him vehemently.

54 Herod found Jesus not guilty also, but, at the instance of his accusers, set him at naught with his men of war and mocked him in a gorgeous robe, and sent him back to Pilate.

55 Then Pilate entered the judgment hall again, and called Jesus and tried him a second time.

56 Pilate saith unto Jesus, Art thou the king of the Jews? Jesus answered him, saying, My kingdom is not of this world. If it were, then would my disciples fight, that I should not be delivered to the Jews.

57 To this end was I born, and for this cause came I into this world, that I should bear witness unto the truth.

58 Pilate saith unto Jesus, What is truth? Then Jesus said, *God's word I have spoken is truth.*

59 Pilate called the chief priests, and the rulers, and the people, and said unto them, Ye have brought this man before me as one that perverteth the people, and behold I have examined him before you and found no fault in him.

60 No, nor yet Herod; for I sent you to him, and lo, he found nothing worthy of death in him.

61 Therefore I will chastise him and release him. But they cried out, Crucify him, crucify him.

62 Then Pilate for the third time said unto them, Why, what evil hath he done?

63 Then they cried out, If thou let this man go, thou art not Cæsar's friend.

64 Whoso maketh himself a king speaketh against Cæsar.

65 Pilate feared Cæsar, and when he heard that, and that he could not prevail, and that a tumult was about to be made, he took water and washed his hands, saying, I am innocent of the blood of this just man. See ye to it. Then they said, His blood be on us and our children. And Pilate delivered Jesus to them to be crucified.

66 Jesus had no advocate except Pilate's wife, Claudia Procula, who sent word to him to have nothing to do with that just man.

67 The soldiers of Pilate took Jesus, and gathered the whole band of soldiers, and put a scarlet robe on him, and a crown of thorns on his head, and a reed in his right hand, and mocked him.

68 They spit on him, and broke the reed over his head; then they led him away to Calvary.

69 There followed a great multitude of people and women which bewailed and lamented. Jesus, turning, said unto them, Daughters of Jerusalem, weep not for me, but weep for yourselves and your children; for desolation will come on you.

70 When they were come to Calvary, there they nailed him to the cross, and crucified him. This was about midday on Friday after the full moon in April, A. D. 33.

71 They parted his raiment and cast lots for it.

72 Jesus, when suffering on the cross, prayed to his Father in heaven, saying, *Father, forgive them; for they know not what they do.*

73 There stood by the cross of Jesus, Mary his aged mother, and his mother's sister Mary the wife of Cleophas, and Mary Magdalene, and his beloved

disciple John, and other women and disciples who came with Jesus out of Galilee.

74 And when Jesus saw his mother and his disciple John, he with tender love committed her to the care of that disciple, and from that day John took her into his own house.

75 Near the ninth hour, or 3 o'clock P. M., Jesus cried and said with a loud voice, My God, my God, why hast thou forsaken me?

76 Jesus next said, I thirst. And they gave him vinegar on a sponge, and he received it.

77 Jesus cried again in a loud voice, *Father, into thy hands I commend my spirit.*

78 Then they gave him wine mingled with myrrh, but he received it not.

79 Then Jesus said, It is finished. And he bowed his head and gave up the ghost.

80 Then the soldiers pierced his side, and forth there came blood and water.

81 Now from twelve to three o'clock P. M. darkness prevailed, and as Jesus gave up the ghost the earth did quake and the rocks were rended, and the vail of the temple was rent.

82 And angels appeared.

83 When the centurion saw these things, he said, Truly this was the Son of God.

84 When the evening was come, there came Joseph, a rich man and an honorable counsellor of Arimathea, and he went boldly to Pilate and asked him for the body of Jesus, that he might bury it.

85 Pilate granted his request, and gave commandment that Jesus' body be delivered to him. And the centurion gave the body of Jesus to Joseph.

86 Then came Nicodemus, a ruler of the Jews,

and they took the body of Jesus and wound it in fine linen clothes with spices.

87 In the place where Jesus was crucified there was a garden, and there was Joseph's own new tomb hewn out in the rock, wherein man was never laid before, and they laid Jesus' body in it, and rolled a great stone to the door of the sepulchre, and departed. And the women were helping and watching.

88 The next day the chief priests and scribes came to Pilate, saying, We remember that Jesus said, After three days I will rise again. Command therefore that the sepulchre be made sure till the third day.

89 Pilate said, Ye have a watch of soldiers: go your way, and make it sure as ye can.

90 So they went and made the sepulchre sure, sealing the great stone and setting the watch.

91 Two thieves were crucified with Jesus. One of them said, We suffer justly; but this man Jesus hath done nothing amiss. And he said unto Jesus, Lord, remember me when thou comest into thy kingdom.

92 And Jesus said unto him, *This day shalt thou be with me in paradise.*

CHAPTER XVII.

His ascension to heaven—His commissions to the women and disciples—Christ afterwards preaches to the spirits in hell—Makes a prison delivery—Conclusion of the whole matter—Love God and keep his commandments in thy strength and manhood as well as in sickness and old age.

1 Then early in the Sabbath, as the day began to dawn, Mary Magdalene, Mary the mother of Jesus, and Mary the mother of James, and Joanna, and Salome, and other women which came with Jesus out of Galilee, came to the sepulchre of Jesus.

2 And behold there was a great earthquake, for the angel of the Lord descended from heaven, and came and rolled the great stone back from the door of the sepulchre, and sat upon it.

3 His countenance was like lightning and his raiment was white as snow.

4 And for fear of him the keepers did shake and became as dead men.

5 The women were affrighted, and the angel answered, and said unto them,

6 Fear not ye; for I know ye seek Jesus of Nazareth, who was crucified. He is not here. Come and see the place where the Lord lay, and go quickly and tell his disciples that he is risen from the dead.

7 And, as commanded by the great angel, they went to the sepulchre, and some of them entered in at the door, and found not the body of the Lord Jesus.

8 They were much perplexed, and behold two angels stood beside them in shining garments, and the women bowed their faces to the earth, when the angels said unto them: Why seek ye the living

among the dead? He is not here, but is risen from the dead. Go tell his disciples.

9 Afterwards others saw another angel, a young man clothed in white, and yet other angels.

10 And as they went to tell his disciples, Mary Magdalene was behind the others, and was weeping. Jesus met them, but withheld their eyes. As he came to Mary, he said, Woman, why weepest thou? Mary answered, Sir, they have taken the body of my Lord. Tell me where they laid him, and I will take him away.

11 Jesus said unto her, Mary. And she turned and said unto him, Master. Then Jesus said to the other women, All hail. And then their eyes were opened and they knew him also, and they all ran to worship him.

12 Jesus commanded them to touch him not, as he had not ascended to the Father; but the women laid hold of his feet and worshiped him.

13 Jesus told them to be not afraid, but go and tell his disciples.

14 Then they went and told his disciples that Jesus had arisen from the dead, and that they had seen a vision of angels, and then had seen Jesus.

15 Peter and John ran to the sepulchre, and found it as the women told them.

16 Other women went to the sepulchre about sunrise, and saw an angel, a young man, sitting on the right side of it.

17 Then that same Sabbath Jesus manifested himself unto two of his apostles as a stranger, expounding the Scriptures, and then as their Lord and Master, and then vanished out of their sight at Emmaus, near Jerusalem.

18 These same two apostles went that same

night to Jerusalem and met the other seven apostles in a room, and told them they had seen Jesus and talked with him, and the doors were shut.

19 And as they spoke, Jesus stood in the midst of them, and they were affrighted, and supposed they had seen a spirit. And he said unto them, Be not afraid. Peace be unto you. It is I.

20 He asked them why they were troubled and why thoughts arose in their hearts.

21 Then he showed them the prints of the nails in his hands and feet, and of the spear in his side, made when he was crucified.

22 He ate broiled fish and honeycomb before them, and said unto them, A spirit hath not flesh and bones as ye see me.

23 Then he opened up their understanding, that they might interpret the Scriptures.

24 Then Jesus appeared unto his disciples at the sea of Galilee, and to many of them and his brethren on the mount in Galilee, where he first preached the gospel of the kingdom of God.

25 He appeared in angel form and also in human form, and convinced the doubting that he was surely arisen from the dead.

26 He was seen by hundreds of honorable men and women, and who knew him personally, after he was crucified, dead, and buried, and these facts were vouched for by them while life lasted, and many of them suffered death rather than retract their witness, or deny their Master and Savior.

27 Jesus remained on this earth about forty days after his crucifixion; and when ascension day was come, which was in May, A. D. 33, he led his disciples out as far as Bethany, about three miles from Jerusalem.

28 And then he showed himself alive after his passion to many of his disciples and brethren.

29 And he saith unto them, Peace be unto you. As my Father sent me, so I send you into the world.

30 Then he breathed on them, and said, Receive ye the Holy Ghost. And then Jesus said unto them, It was meet that I should have suffered and have died and to arise from the dead on the third day, that repentance, and observance of the commandments, and remission of sins should be preached in all nations, beginning at Jerusalem. And ye are witnesses of these things.

31 Then he saith to the women, Go to my brethren and tell them I ascend to my Father and your Father, and to my God and your God.

32 And to his disciples he saith, All power in heaven and earth is given unto me.

33 Go ye therefore into all the world, and preach the gospel to every creature. He that believeth and is baptized shall be saved; but he that believeth not shall be damned. (See Mark xvi. 15.)

34 Go ye therefore and teach all nations, baptizing them in the name of the Father, Son, and Holy Ghost; teaching them to observe all things I have commanded you: and lo, I am with you always, even unto the end of the world. (Matt. xxviii. 19.)

35 Then Jesus lifted up his hands and blessed his disciples and the world; and as he was blessing them, he was slowly carried up into heaven, and a cloud received him out of sight.

36 And two angels stood beside them in white apparel, and while Christ's disciples were still looking up into heaven, they said unto them, Why stand

ye gazing up to heaven? This same Jesus, which is taken from you up into heaven, shall again return to you as ye have seen him go up to heaven.

37 And the disciples worshiped Jesus, and returned to Jerusalem with great joy, and were continually in the temple praising and blessing God, till they began to preach the gospel again.

38 Soon after our Lord and Master was crucified and ascended to heaven, and in the lifetime of his apostle Peter, he went from the right hand of the power of God, and preached the gospel to the spirits in the prison of hell.

39 His mission was to preach the gospel to the dead, that they might be judged according to men in the flesh, but live according to God in the spirit.

40 His mission to the spirits in prison, who were sometimes disobedient in this life, was to bring them to God.

41 He preached his gospel to the sinners in the prison of hell; they heard it; they believed it; and they repented and were restored to reason, and they remembered their Father in the kingdom of heaven.

42 And on the invitation of our Lord, they arose up and went with him and his holy angels to their Father in heaven.

43 He met them with the same compassion and joy with which he met his prodigal son, and gave them the same royal reception, feast, and banquet.

44 And he rewarded them for every good deed they had done in this life; their evil deeds had been destroyed by repentance.

45 It was Christ's mission to them to bring them to God.

46 Our Lord and Master preached the gospel and gave up the ghost for all, the just for the unjust, that he might bring them all unto God, in due season.

47 He is gone to heaven and is on the right hand of God, angels and authorities and powers being made subject unto him. Hear ye him.

48 For blessed are the dead which die in the Lord from henceforth. Yea, saith the Spirit, that they may rest from their labors; and their works do follow them.

49 And the Spirit and the Bride say, Come. And let him that heareth say, Come. And let him that is athirst come. And whosoever will, let him come and take of the waters of life freely.

50 And every creature which is in heaven, and on the earth, and under the earth, and such as are in the sea, and all that are in them, John Divine heard saying, Blessing, and honor, and glory, and power be unto him that sitteth on the throne, and unto the Lord for ever and ever.

51 The commandments, the promises and revelations of God to man, are written in the starry heavens, and in the earth, and in the hearts of men.

52 And the world has no excuse for unbelief nor for willful sins.

53 Let us hear the conclusion of the whole matter. *Love God and keep his commandments;* for this is the whole duty of man.

54 For God shall bring every work into judgment, with every secret thing, whether it be good, or whether it be evil.

55 Remember now thy Creator in the days of thy youth, and of thy strength, and of thy manhood,

and before the feebleness of sickness and old age death shall come nigh unto you.

56 And receive a full reward in heaven your good conduct in this world.

AMEN.

www.ingramcontent.com/pod-product-compliance
Lightning Source LLC
Chambersburg PA
CBHW022143160426
43197CB00009B/1415